An Employer's and Engineer's Guide to the FIDIC Conditions of Contract

This book's companion website is at
www.wiley.com/go/robinsonfidic-employer and offers invaluable resources to freely download, adapt and use:

- Model letters for use by the Employer
- Model letters for use by the Contractor
- Sample Interim Payment Certificate
- Model Form for Submissions to the Engineer
- Model Form of Engineer's Order for Varied Works
- Model Form of Daywork/Daily Record Sheets

An Employer's and Engineer's Guide to the FIDIC Conditions of Contract

Michael D. Robinson
Independent Consulting Engineer

A John Wiley & Sons, Ltd., Publication

This edition first published 2013
© 2013 John Wiley & Sons, Ltd

Wiley-Blackwell is an imprint of John Wiley & Sons, formed by the merger of Wiley's global Scientific, Technical and Medical business with Blackwell Publishing.

Registered Office
John Wiley & Sons, Ltd, The Atrium, Southern Gate, Chichester, West Sussex, PO19 8SQ, UK

Editorial Offices
9600 Garsington Road, Oxford, OX4 2DQ, UK
The Atrium, Southern Gate, Chichester, West Sussex, PO19 8SQ, UK
2121 State Avenue, Ames, Iowa 50014-8300, USA

For details of our global editorial offices, for customer services and for information about how to apply for permission to reuse the copyright material in this book please see our website at www.wiley.com/wiley-blackwell.

The right of the author to be identified as the author of this work has been asserted in accordance with the UK Copyright, Designs and Patents Act 1988.

All rights reserved. No part of this publication may be reproduced, stored in a retrieval system, or transmitted, in any form or by any means, electronic, mechanical, photocopying, recording or otherwise, except as permitted by the UK Copyright, Designs and Patents Act 1988, without the prior permission of the publisher.

Designations used by companies to distinguish their products are often claimed as trademarks. All brand names and product names used in this book are trade names, service marks, trademarks or registered trademarks of their respective owners. The publisher is not associated with any product or vendor mentioned in this book. This publication is designed to provide accurate and authoritative information in regard to the subject matter covered. It is sold on the understanding that the publisher is not engaged in rendering professional services. If professional advice or other expert assistance is required, the services of a competent professional should be sought.

Limit of Liability/Disclaimer of Warranty: While the publisher and author have used their best efforts in preparing this book, they make no representations or warranties with the respect to the accuracy or completeness of the contents of this book and specifically disclaim any implied warranties of merchantability or fitness for a particular purpose. It is sold on the understanding that the publisher is not engaged in rendering professional services and neither the publisher nor the author shall be liable for damages arising herefrom. If professional advice or other expert assistance is required, the services of a competent professional should be sought.

Library of Congress Cataloging-in-Publication Data
Robinson, Michael D., (Consulting engineer)
  An employer's and engineer's guide to the FIDIC conditions of contract / Michael D. Robinson.
     pages   cm
  Includes indexes.
  ISBN 978-1-118-38560-9 (cloth)
1. Construction contracts. 2. Engineering contracts. 3. Architectural contracts. 4. Standardized terms of contract. 5. FIDIC form of contract. I. Title.
  K891.B8R6136 2013
  343.07′8624–dc23
                                                    2012040308

A catalogue record for this book is available from the British Library.

Wiley also publishes its books in a variety of electronic formats. Some content that appears in print may not be available in electronic books.

ISBN: 978-1-118-38560-9

Set in 10/12pt Sabon by SPi Publisher Services, Pondicherry, India

1 2013

Contents

Preface   vii
Acknowledgements and Dedication   xi

Chapter 1	The Employer and the FIDIC Conditions of Contract for Construction (CONS) – 'The Red Book'	1
Chapter 2	The Engineer and the FIDIC Conditions of Contract for Construction (CONS) – 'The Red Book'	71

Appendices   145

Appendix A	Conditions of Contract for Plant and Design-Build 1999 (P & DB) 'The Yellow Book'	147
Appendix B	Conditions of Contract for EPC/Turnkey Projects (EPCT) 'The Silver Book'	150
Appendix C	Other FIDIC Publications	151
Appendix D	Employer's Claims under a CONS Contract	153
Appendix E	Contractor's Claims under a CONS Contract	154
Appendix F	Preparation of Interim Payment Certificates	156
Appendix G	Model Form for Submissions to the Engineer for Approval and/or Consent	160
Appendix H	Model Form of Engineer's Order for Varied Works	161
Appendix I	Model Form of Daywork/Daily Record Sheets	162
Appendix J	Model Letters for Use by the Employer	164
Appendix K	Model Letters for Use by the Engineer	175

Introduction to Indexes   205
Index of Sub-Clauses (FIDIC System)   206
Index of Sub-Clauses (sorted according to FIDIC Clause numbering system)   212

Preface

The Conditions of Contract prepared by FIDIC have for many years had no rival as the standard form of choice for use in the international construction industry.

Traditionally in the standard FIDIC forms the Engineer was given an authorative role, enabling him to make informed judgements concerning the conduct and execution of projects with a large measure of independence from the Employer. From time to time FIDIC updated these standard forms, continuing to maintain the traditional role of the Engineer, culminating in the 4th Edition 1987 (reprinted 1992).

These standard forms described the duties, responsibilities and obligations of not only the Employer and the Contractor, the signatories of the Contract, but also the Engineer, engaged by the Employer to supervise the execution of the Contract. Not infrequently the Engineer was also engaged by the Employer to execute the design of the project under the terms of a separate agreement.

However, throughout the 1980s and 1990s discernible changes developed in the international construction industry. Employers increasingly became involved in the day-by-day administration of projects, thereby restricting the powers of the Engineer to act independently of the parties. This trend was amplified as more projects were financed by international financing agencies who, understandably, sought greater control over the budgetary aspects of the projects for which they were providing finance. The consequential diminution of the power and authority of the Engineer had the effect of disturbing the allocation of risk between the Employer and the Contractor, and, as many contractors perceived, to their disadvantage.

A further development was the steady increase in international trade, which for the construction industry has resulted in more companies undertaking contracts outside their own national borders.

Disputes have long been endemic to the construction industry. The participation of more and more companies of differing nationalities in projects outside their own borders inevitably increased the number of disputes arising for a multitude of reasons. Engineers and Contractors were not always familiar with the operation of a FIDIC-based contract. Employers, well used to their own national systems of contracting practice and national laws, were faced with having to deal with contracts based on unfamiliar FIDIC forms. As a consequence, the number of disputes increased markedly.

A key feature of the dispute resolution procedure contained in the FIDIC 4th Edition 1987, Sub-Clause 67.1 'Engineer's Decision' was the power and authority of the Engineer to make independent judgements in respect of Contractor's claims. Consequently, as the independence of the Engineer diminished as a result of the increasing direct involvement of the Employer, the value of the Engineer's Decision was increasingly challenged by contractors, with the result that more and more disputes were referred to arbitration.

Few in the construction industry regard arbitration as a satisfactory means of resolving disputes. Arbitration is a lengthy and expensive process. With a more disciplined and flexible approach, solutions may have been negotiated without arbitration. A contractor suffers as a consequence, because he is unable to foresee the outcome of the arbitration and his cash-flow is uncertain and damaged as a consequence of lengthy arbitration. This uncertainty is also detrimental to the Employer's interest.

Against this background FIDIC undertook a major review of their standard forms which in many aspects departed significantly from the forms then in use. Following extensive consultations, a new suite of contract forms was issued in 1999:

(i) *CONS – Conditions of Contract for Construction ('The Red Book')*, which FIDIC recommends for use on building or engineering works designed by the Employer or his representative, the Engineer

(ii) *P & DB – Conditions of Contract for Plant and Design-Build ('The Yellow Book')*, which FIDIC recommends for the provision of electrical and/or mechanical plant and for the design and execution of building or engineering works to be designed by the Contractor in accordance with the Employer's requirements

(iii) *EPCT – Conditions of Contract for EPC/Turnkey Projects ('The Silver Book')*, which FIDIC recommends for the provision of a process or power plant on a turnkey project

A fourth Conditions of Contract entitled 'Short Form of Contract' ('The Green Book') intended for use on contracts involving simple or repetitive work, was also issued by FIDIC in 1999.

In the intervening years FIDIC have expanded the range of Contract Forms to include:

(iv) *Conditions of Contract for Construction, MDB Harmonised Edition – 'The Pink Book'*

    Version 1   Published May 2005
    Version 2   Published March 2006
    Version 3   Published June 2010

A significant part of financing for internationally tendered projects is provided by one or more of the various international financing agencies, such as World Bank. These agencies had growing reservations that funding provided was subject to mismanagement, which encouraged corruption and financial losses. Eventually there was common agreement that the required financial controls could be met by the introduction of a modified form of The Red Book (CONS), which essentially allowed for greater access to the financial records of the Contractors for audit purposes. Other aspects of The Red Book (CONS) are not materially altered in this Harmonised Edition.

(v) *DBO – Conditions of Contract. Design. Build. Operate ('The GoldBook')*, published 2008. Prior to the issue of these Conditions of Contract, the steady increase in the number of DBO contracts was catered for by modifications and variations to the available standard forms of contract. Each contract was individually prepared and negotiated, often incorporating elements of other FIDIC forms. The addition of the DBO Conditions of Contract to the new suite of contract forms will assist reduce uncertainties and errors.

(vi) *Construction 1999 Red Book Subcontract 4th Edition 2006*. This update of subcontract forms, which is now compatible with the new suite of contract forms, is a welcome addition to the FIDIC suite of contract forms.

In the preparation of the new suite of contracts, FIDIC continued with the use of the English language as the language of interpretation, although FIDIC does provide translations into a number of major languages. The availability of these translations can be viewed on the FIDIC bookshop website. In retaining the use of the English language, FIDIC took the opportunity to ensure that all of the forms in the new suite were written in modern English and not the more legalistic English used in the forms of Contract issued prior to 1999. Nonetheless, engineers with a lesser command of the English language have tended to find it difficult to assimilate the requirements, obligations and duties contained in the FIDIC forms.

The FIDIC forms of the Rainbow Suite (excluding The Green Book) are arranged in twenty primary clauses with a total of 158 sub-clauses (in The Red Book) and consequently it takes practice and experience to be able to draw together all the sub-clauses relating to a particular issue. An important example is the presentation of an individual claim by a contractor. The Contractor will be required to make reference not only to the clause or sub-clause that permits the Contractor to make the claim, but also to Sub-Clauses 3.5, 8.4 and 20.1 which are widely separated in the FIDIC forms. It is important that professional users of the FIDIC forms make themselves familiar with the general philosophy adopted by the FIDIC Committee, who were charged with the preparation of these forms.

This book has the aim to assist the Employer and the Engineer and his site staff manage difficulties which frequently arise on typical international contracts using the FIDIC forms. Since the majority of FIDIC-based contracts use The Red Book (CONS) standard forms, this book is focused on those forms. Supplementary comments are included in Appendix A in respect of The Yellow Book (P & DB), recommended for use where the Contractor has a design responsibility. Brief comments on other forms of contract are included in Appendices B and C.

This book is not intended to be a review of the legal aspects of FIDIC-based contracts. Legal advice should be obtained where appropriate, particularly if the Contractor has little or no knowledge of the laws of the country of execution.

It is hoped that this book will assist all site staff in supervisory roles to prevent problems arising, rather than spend considerable time and energy dealing with problems once they have arisen.

It is particularly important that all parties adhere to the procedural requirements given in the Contract and not to make expedient decisions, which eventually can damage site relationships and affect the execution of the Contract.

It is recommended that the reader gives consideration to the purchase of a copy of 'The FIDIC Contracts Guide', published in 2000, which provides valuable additional commentary on the use and interpretation of the referenced FIDIC forms.

Acknowledgements

The author is grateful to the Fèdèration Internationale des Ingénieurs-Conseils (FIDIC) for permission to quote extracts from the Conditions of Contract for Construction ('The Red Book') and the FIDIC Contracts Guide. All quoted extracts from these publications are given in italics wherever they occur.

In this book, the Employer, the Engineer, the Contractor and Subcontractors are referred to in the masculine gender in conformity with standard FIDIC Practice. The author wishes to emphasise that the book is intended to address female readers on an equal basis with their male colleagues and that the use of the masculine gender is for practical reasons only.

Dedication

This book is dedicated to my wife Monika, without whose contribution, encouragement and support nothing would have been achieved; to my sons Paul, Simon and Tristan, who have so enriched my life; and to all those who have shared with me many long arduous days working on construction projects worldwide.

You may also be interested in...

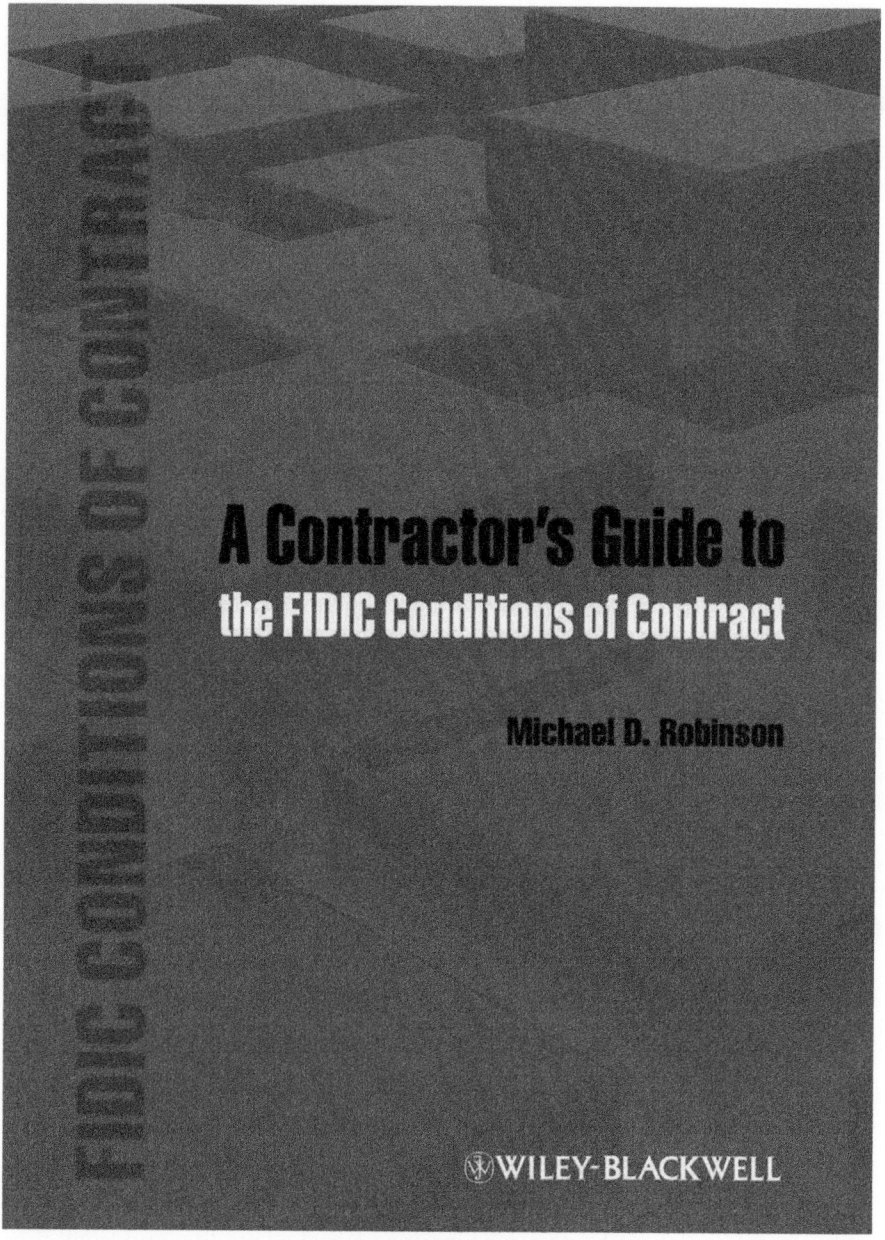

978-0-470-65764-5
£56.50, 272 pages, Hardcover
Published April 2011

The companion website is at www.wiley.com/go/robinsonfidic and offers invaluable resources for the site-based contractor to freely download and adapt: model form for submissions to the engineer for approval and/or consent; model form of daywork / daily record sheets; and sample model letters for use by the contractor.

Chapter 1

The Employer and the FIDIC Conditions of Contract for Construction (CONS) – 'The Red Book'

Chapter 1

The Employer and the FIDIC Conditions of Contract for Construction (CONS) – The Red Book

Clause 1 General Provisions

1.0

Much of the primary planning and organisation of a project is necessarily defined and arranged by the Employer in the pre-tender stage. Consequently the quality of this work will have a significant effect on the execution of the project. The FIDIC Contracts Guide, under the headings of Procurement and Project Documentation, provides valuable guidance to the Employer in respect of this primary planning and organisation.

The FIDIC Conditions of Contract consequently reflects the decisions reached by the Employer in the pre-tender stage and proceeds to define the duties and responsibilities of the Parties and the allocation of risk between them.

The Conditions of Contract incorporated in the tender documents and in the Contract Agreement include a significant number of Clauses and Sub-Clauses the contents of which refer to matters which have (or should have) been addressed by the Employer in the preparation of the tender documents.

The number of issues to be addressed by the Employer during the construction period are somewhat less than might be apparent from a first reading of the Conditions of Contract. These issues are identified and discussed in this chapter.

1.1 Definitions

This sub-clause provides definitions of approximately 65 words and expressions that are used in the Conditions of Contract. *With the exception of the words 'day' and 'year', these defined words and expressions are identifiable by the use of capital initial letters.*

Consequently, in any submission or correspondence it is important to use the capitalised form of the words and expressions if that is what is precisely intended by the writer.

The FIDIC Contracts Guide (p. 339–346) provides a glossary (dictionary) of words and phrases which are in common use in the civil engineering and building industry. This glossary does not amplify or replace the definitions given in this Sub-Clause 1.1, but the consistent use of the definitions contained in this glossary is useful to ensure clarity on a given topic.

The Employer has the responsibility for the correctness and consistency of the Contract Documents and may find it necessary to introduce additional expressions or words into the text which require appropriate definitions to be added. There are a significant number of words which are loosely used in the construction industry, such as 'variation order', 'working drawings',

---

An Employer's and Engineer's Guide to the FIDIC Conditions of Contract, First Edition. Michael D. Robinson.
© 2013 John Wiley & Sons, Ltd. Published 2013 by John Wiley & Sons, Ltd.

which are not defined in these Conditions of Contract and consequently should not be used if other more appropriate definitions are already available.

Sub-Clause 1.1.1   Contract

In the preparation of the tender documents the Employer or the Employer's personnel will need to identify any further documents (in addition to those already indicated) for eventual inclusion in the Contract Agreement.

Sub-Clause 1.1.1.3   Letter of Acceptance
In many jurisdictions the Employer who is a government department or agency may be prohibited by law from entering into a contract by means of a Letter of Acceptance. In such circumstances, to conclude a binding contract will require a complete contract document to be prepared and signed by the Parties.

Sub-Clause 1.1.1.6   Drawings
The Employer is required to provide the Drawings of the Works to the Contractor for execution. The Contractor is required to provide his own workshop or working drawings which will provide detail of how he will execute the Works. Unless specifically stated, the Contractor does not have a duty to modify or correct drawings provided by the Employer. Indeed he may be prohibited from doing so by the applicable law and by the terms of the project insurances.

Sub-Clause 1.1.1.9   Appendix to Tender
Omissions and errors may occur in the preparation of the Appendix to Tender. The Contractor may identify some of these omissions and errors in the preparation of his Tender, but a detailed check of this document is highly recommended before issuing the same to tenderers.

Sub-Clause 1.1.2.4   Engineer
It is intended that the Engineer is named in the Appendix to Tender (for further commentary see Clause 3).

Sub-Clause 1.1.2.6   Employer's Personnel
It is to be noted that this term includes the Engineer and his assistants. The use of the term 'Personnel' does not imply that the concerned people are necessarily employees of the Employer.

Sub-Clause 1.1.2.9   DAB (Dispute Adjudication Board)
The Employer is required to decide the composition of the DAB within the tender documents, as part of the cost thereof has to be included in the Contractor's tender offer. (It is to be noted that the MDB Harmonised Edition, the 'Pink Book', uses the term 'Dispute Board' [DB], in substitution for 'Dispute Adjudication Board' [DAB].)

1.2 Interpretation

This sub-clause contains legal statements confirming (except where the context requires otherwise)

(a) words indicating one gender include all genders
(b) words indicating the singular also include the plural and vice-versa
(c) 'Agreements' are to be recorded in writing. Verbal agreements made by the Parties should be recorded in writing. A failure to record verbal agreements can cause difficulties at a later stage particularly if there are changes in personnel
(d) where something is stated to be 'written' or 'in writing' this shall result in a permanent record. Reference may be made to the authorised means of communication identified in Sub-Clause 1.3.

1.3 Communications

In the preparation of the tender documents the Employer is required to identify the authorised means of communication between the Parties.

Sub-paragraph 1.3(a) provides for the following means of communication:

- in writing and delivered by hand. This remains an important means of communication where the Parties are normally in close physical proximity or where the communication is bulky or of a physical nature or where the document is of sufficient value or importance that warrants a personal delivery. The use of a formal mail transmission book is highly recommended
- by electronic transmission using any of the agreed systems of electronic transmission. In particular if e-mail communications are not permitted or are restricted, this needs to be clarified.

Both Parties should ensure that only authorised staff members are allowed to formally communicate and that the other Party is informed in writing of the limitations of any delegated authority.

1.4 Law and Language

The Employer is required to define both the applicable law and the language of communication in the Appendix to Tender. Invariably the applicable law will be that of the country where the contract is to be executed. For all contracts, where the Employer is a state organisation or other public body, the use of local law is likely to be mandatory.

Exceptionally and particularly, where both the Employer and the Contractor are non-resident in the country of execution and where the commercial laws of the country of execution are not well developed, the Parties may elect to specify the use of the laws of a more developed country.

Where the Employer is a state organisation or other public body, the Employer is likely to require that all communications from the Engineer or the

Contractor are provided in the official language of the country of execution. It has become a standard practice for the Engineer and the Contractor, when writing to the Employer in the official language of the country of execution, to also provide a simultaneous translation into the language of the Contract.

1.5 Priority of Documents

A listing of standard documents and their priorities is given in the Conditions of Contract. The Employer has the responsibility to ensure that this model listing is suitably upgraded in the final Contract document to reflect the titles and content of the actual documents included in the tender package together with any relevant documentation provided by the Contractor with his tender offer.

Further, the conclusions of any post-tender negotiations between the Employer and the prospective Contractor need to be formally agreed and included in the Contract as a separate document of the highest priority.

1.6 Contract Agreement

The standard FIDIC Conditions of Contract provides that a Letter of Agreement shall be provided by the Employer and within a period of 28 days a Contract Agreement shall be drawn up and finalised between the Parties. The Employer is responsible for all taxes and other charges which may arise in the preparation of the Contract Agreement. If a Letter of Agreement is not required, the time interval between tender date and the date of signing a Contract Agreement is to be stated in the Instructions to Tenderers.

1.7 Assignment

Neither Party (Employer or Contractor) is permitted to assign or transfer the whole or any part of the Contract without the prior agreement of the other Party.

Should the Employer receive a request for assignment from the Contractor, legal advice should be sought particularly with reference to key contract documents such as the Performance Security, Advance Payment Guarantees, and Insurances.

1.8 Care and Supply of Documents

The Employer (not the Engineer) is required to provide to the Contractor two copies of the Contract which typically includes all those documents (including Drawings) which are identified in Sub-Clause 1.5. In addition two copies of any subsequent drawings are to be provided by the Employer to the Contractor. Since these subsequent drawings are most likely to be produced by the Engineer, the Employer may also delegate responsibility for their distribution to the Engineer.

This sub-clause makes no mention of the need for Drawings to be provided in a reproducible format which would not only facilitate general distribution, but would also be of considerable benefit in the anticipated eventual preparation of so-called 'as-built' drawings.

The Contractor is required to provide to the Engineer (not the Employer) six copies of each of the Contractor's Documents. The Contractor's Documents would importantly include submittals requiring the Engineer's consent. The Contractor should seek clarification from the Engineer if a full submittal of all six copies is required at the submittal for approval stage. It is possible that only a full submittal is required once the documents are approved.

It may be mutually convenient if documentation, particularly drawings, can be passed electronically between the Parties. This should be discussed between the Parties at the earliest opportunity, as this would for example facilitate the production of 'as-built' drawings.

1.9 Delayed Drawings and Instructions

Each Party has a general obligation to notify the other Party when it becomes aware of a technical defect or error in the Documents. Each Party has the implied duty of care to the other and the applicable law may also impose this duty.

The sub-clause refers only to the technical defects or errors (and not those of a financial or other nature) the consequences of which may give rise to a Variation to the Contract as described in Sub-Clause 13.1.

The Contractor is required to give reasonable notice to the Engineer if there are likely to be delays or disruption caused by a late supply of drawings or instructions. The notice shall give details of the requested drawings or instructions, when it is required and the likely consequences if the drawing or instructions are delayed. Should the Works be delayed, then the Contractor, having given notice in accordance with Sub-Clause 20.1, shall be entitled to an extension of time and to payment of Cost plus profit.

1.10 Employer's Use of the Contractor's Documents

The Contractor retains intellectual property rights in the Contractor's Documents and other design documents made by (or on behalf of) the Contractor.

At the signing of the Contract the Contractor is deemed to have given the Employer a non-terminable transferable non-exclusive royalty free licence to copy, use or communicate the Contractor's Documents including making and using modifications of them.

The licence applies throughout the normal working life of the relevant part of the Works and entitles any person in possession of the relevant part of the Works to use the Contractor's Documents to complete, operate, adjust, repair, etc., the Works.

The Employer is entitled to use computer programs and other software supplied by the Contractor under the Contract, but is not entitled to use such information for similar works.

The FIDIC Contracts Guide gives a reminder that the term 'Contractor's Documents' refers to documents which the Contractor was required to supply under the terms of the Contract and not to other documents which may have been supplied by the Contractor. Any permission given by the Contractor is to be given in writing.

1.11 Contractor's Use of Employer's Documents

This sub-clause is effectively a mirror image of Sub-Clause 1.10.

The Employer retains the copyright and other intellectual property rights in the Specification, the Drawings and other documents made by (or on behalf of) the Employer, which would encompass drawings provided by the Engineer.

The Contractor is permitted to copy and use these documents at his own cost, but is not permitted to communicate the same to third parties except as necessary for the purposes of the Contract. Consequently a Contractor is permitted to provide copies of these documents to suppliers and subcontractors, but not for example to the media for publicity purposes.

1.12 Confidential Details

The Contractor is required '*to disclose all such confidential and other information as the Engineer may reasonably require in order to verify the Contractor's compliance with the Contract*'.

The FIDIC Contracts Guide explains that '*although the Employer might like to have details of Plant and other parts of the Works to be supplied to him, Contractors and Subcontractors will wish to keep confidential certain processes which they regard as trade secrets*'.

1.13 Compliance with Statutes, Regulations and Laws

Although the Contractor, in performing the Works, is required to comply with applicable law, certain duties are placed on the Employer.

- The Employer has the duty to obtain the planning and similar permissions for the Permanent Works. Major projects may require special legislation and cross border arrangements with neighbouring countries. The Employer indemnifies the Contractor in respect of any failure by him to obtain these permissions. The Contractor is required to comply with the applicable law.
- The Contractor, not the Employer, is required to give all notices, pay all taxes, duties and fees and obtain all permits, licences and approvals, as

required by the applicable laws relating to the execution of the Contract. It will be noted that the term 'Law' is a defined term (Sub-Clause 1.1.6.5) and in addition to national or state statutes and laws also includes regulations and by-laws of any legally constituted public authority.

Any exceptions to these general obligations of the Contractor can be specified and included in the Particular Conditions of Contract. In some instances there may be advantages to the Employer if he were to arrange and pay for key services to the Site in advance of the Contractor starting work. A prime example would be the supply of electrical power and/or water to a location close to the Site.

1.14 Joint and Several Liability

In order to limit individual risk and to share resources and expertise, it is a common practice, particularly for larger complex projects, for the Contractor to consist of two or more companies who have jointly tendered as a joint venture (or a consortium or other unincorporated grouping).

The Instructions to Tenderers, in authorising tenders from joint ventures, will have specified in detail the terms and conditions governing the acceptability of these joint ventures.

The Instructions to Tenderers will contain a reference to this Sub-Clause 1.14. Thus, although the acceptability of a joint venture will have been dealt with in detail as part of the tender process, this sub-clause serves to define the crucial legal status of the joint venture executing the Contract:

- All participants in the joint venture are deemed to be jointly and severally liable to the Employer for the performance of the Contract.
- The business of the joint venture will likely be conducted by a committee who will nominate a leader authorised to formally represent them in dealings with the Employer.
- The Contractor (joint venture) is not allowed to alter its composition without the prior consent of the Employer. Changes may be inevitable if a member of the joint venture is unable to continue. In such cases the remaining partners are obliged to accept responsibility for the share of the failing party. Either the remaining joint-venturers will agree a re-arrangement of their respective shareholdings or will seek a replacement partner. Any changes require the consent of the Employer.

Clause 2 The Employer

2.1 Right of Access to the Site

The Employer has the primary obligation to provide the Contractor with access to the Site and possession thereof within the time(s) stated in the Appendix to Tender.

If it is the Employer's intention that the Contractor is not to be given exclusive access to and possession of the Site, then any restrictions and limitations have to be stated in the tender documents in order to allow contractors an opportunity to make due allowance in their tender offers. Any restrictions introduced after the signing of the contract are likely to meet with an adverse reaction from the Contractor.

Should the Employer's overall project planning necessitate that the Site and access thereto be shared between two or more contractors (or the Employer's own organisation for non- contractual purposes), then the Employer will need to decide which party will operate common services, including security and maintenance of the access to the Site.

As part of the handover process it is recommended that the Site and access thereto be formally inspected by the Employer, the Contractor and – if available – the Engineer. The condition of the Site and access should be formally recorded (a video record would be beneficial). Not uncommonly, unattended sites are frequently used as illegal dump sites by others. The cost of removal of such illegal material would be to the Employer's expense if the material was dumped after the date of tender and prior to handover of the Site to the Contractor.

On inspection the Site and access may be further obstructed by buildings or other structures which cannot be cleared due to a lack of requisition or other legal prevention. Should limited obstructions be noted during the inspection, the Employer and the Contractor have the possibility to agree for the Works to commence with the obstruction to be removed by an agreed later date. This solution should prove less costly and minimise delays compared with the alternative of delaying commencement.

If no time for handover is given in the Appendix to Tender, then the Employer is required to make the necessary handovers to correspond with the Contractor's programme submitted under Sub-Clause 8.3. This alternative procedure is not without its hazards, as the Contractor may take some time to prepare the programme (Sub-Clause 8.3 allows the Contractor up to 28 days to prepare and submit the programme). As a consequence, the precise date for handover of the Site can become imprecise and may lead to unforeseen delays.

Experienced contractors will as a matter of course mobilise as quickly as possible and use the initial stages of a contract to set up their site establishment, including the setting up of offices, etc., the bringing to site of the plant, setting out and site clearance, all of which can take place with limited resources and minimal supervision.

It is a regrettable fact that a disproportionate number of delays and claims arise in the opening stages of many projects as a direct consequence of delayed or disturbed site handovers. Self-evidently the timely handover of the Site and the provision of site access is a mutual goal that both the Employer and the Contractor have every interest to strive to achieve.

The wording of this sub-clause requires only that the Employer grants the Contractor the right of access to the Site. The assumption is that there is already an existing practical access or a route which can be adequately improved by the Contractor. Unless there is a specific entitlement elsewhere in the Contract, this Sub-Clause 2.1 does not require the Employer to provide an access route suitable for the Contractor's needs. If the Site is totally surrounded by lands owned by third parties, the Contract should clarify how the Contractor will be granted right of access across such lands.

Extensive sites, such as lengthy road rehabilitation projects, require special considerations. To minimise and control disruption to road users, the Employer may consider handing over the existing road in lengths of approximately 5–10 kilometres, with corresponding diversion lengths. Additional lengths for rehabilitation would be released to the Contractor corresponding to the lengths successfully rehabilitated and available for use by the travelling public. The Employer will need to establish a policy for the taking over of the completed lengths of road. The policy needs to be described in the tender documents and subsequently in the Contract Documents. A taking over represents a transfer of risk from the Contractor to the Engineer and has a number of implications, not least a reduction in the Contractor's insurance obligations.

If the Site is not provided to the Contractor by the due date, then, subject to compliance with the requirements of Sub-Clause 20.1, he is entitled to claim additional compensation and extension of time for completion in accordance with the provisions of Sub-Clause 8.4.

Extraordinary long delays by the Employer in providing the Site and access thereto may entitle the Contractor to terminate the Contract.

2.2 Permits, Licences or Approvals

This sub-clause requires the Employer (wherever he is able) to provide reasonable assistance to the Contractor upon his request:

(a) *'by obtaining copies of the Laws of the Country which are relevant but are not readily available…'*. Assistance in this instance would be especially useful in the preparation of tenders and during the days immediately following commencement when the Contractor is actively establishing himself on site. Official translations would be invaluable.

and

(b) *'for the Contractor's applications for any permits, licences or approvals required by the Laws of the Country*
   (i) *which the Contractor is required to obtain under Sub-Clause 1.13'*. These applications would typically extend to:
- building permits
- design approvals

- compliance with local authority regulations including accesses, road use
- legalisation of vehicles, taxes
- compliance with the relevant labour laws

(ii) for the delivery of Goods including clearance through customs.

In many tightly regulated countries the Contractor is likely to require the close support of the Employer to import Goods through customs. This is especially important if the Employer is a state organisation and the Contract permits the Contractor to import Goods free of customs duties and taxes. Duty free importation normally requires pre-authorisation by the government ministry responsible for customs affairs. Consequently the Employer (assumed also to be a state organisation) is required to ensure that all necessary arrangements are in place before the Contractor commences importation. Delayed importation will likely delay the progress of the Works and cause additional cost to the Contractor for which he can be expected to make claim for reimbursement, particularly if he has been obliged to make a temporary customs payment pending clarification of his contracted duty free status.

Sensitive items, including the importation of explosives, will need special arrangements for their importation, handling and storage. Although the Contractor is responsible for arranging matters, the support of the Employer will be invaluable in dealing with the appropriate authorities.

(iii) for the export of Contractor's equipment when it is removed from the Site.

Having obtained the consent of the Engineer to remove items of the Contractor's Equipment from Site in accordance with Sub-Clause 4.17, the Contractor may decide either

- elect to transfer the Equipment to another State-financed project within the country also with duty free status. In addition to obtaining the authority of the Ministry of Finance to make the transfer, the documentary requirements of the Employer and his counterpart on the receiving project will also have to be met.
- to transfer the Equipment to another project within the country which does not have duty free status. The Contractor will be required to regularise the transfer from temporary importation status to final importation status with the Ministry of Finance. In order to ensure that there is no conflict with the terms of the initial duty-free importation, the Employer is likely to require evidence of those transfers.
- to sell unwanted items of Contractor's Equipment to third parties within the country. Should the cost of transportation on re-exportation be uneconomical relative to the value of the Contractor's Equipment, the Contractor may seek permission to dispose of the Contractor's Equipment locally. These items may also be of interest to the Employer for his own operations.

Again the Contractor will be required to regularise the transfer from temporary importation status to final importation status and the Employer may wish to be kept informed of the Contractor's intentions.
- to re-export the Contractor's Equipment. The Contractor has the responsibility to ensure that paperwork governing the original duty-free importation is correctly reconciled with re-exportation.

2.3   Employer's Personnel

This sub-clause confirms that the Employer is responsible for ensuring that the Employer's Personnel and the Employer's other contractors on the Site will co-operate with the Contractor in fulfilling his duties described in Sub-Clause 4.6 (Co-operation) and will take similar action to support the Contractor's efforts in respect of safety procedures (Sub-Clause 4.8) and protection of the environment (Sub-Clause 4.18).

Although not specifically identified in this sub-clause, it is reasonable to assume that the Employer will ensure that the Employer's Personnel co-operate with the Contractor in respect of security of the Site (Sub-Clause 4.22).

The FIDIC Contracts Guide confirms that the term 'Employer's Personnel' includes the Engineer and his staff.

2.4   Employer's Financial Arrangement

At the time of tender the Contractor will have a general understanding of the means by which the Employer intends to finance the execution of the Works. Where the Employer is a state authority, it is quite possible that the funding will be provided by an international financial institution, such as the World Bank. Understandably these institutions require a strict financial control of the funds provided. As a consequence the Engineer is routinely prevented from agreeing any additional payment without the prior authorisation of the Employer.

Given the unpredictable nature of many building and civil engineering projects, there is a distinct risk that the amount of available funding may be inadequate to complete the Works as planned without the injection of further funding. Often this additional funding cannot be obtained within an ideal time frame, with the net result that the Contractor is not paid within the stated time periods.

The situation is exacerbated if additional work has to be performed which necessitates additional payment to the Contractor in accordance with the procedures given in Clause 13, Variations and Adjustments. The Contractor will become concerned if payments rightly due are delayed for lengthy periods, particularly if he himself is under pressure from his own bankers. It would be hoped that a positive relationship between the Employer and the Contractor will allow matters to be discussed and a mutually satisfactory solution developed to expedite payments due.

However, if the Contractor became seriously concerned of the Employer's ability to pay the amounts due under the terms of the Contract, this Clause 2.4 entitles the Contractor to request the Employer to *'provide reasonable evidence that financial arrangements have been made and are being maintained, which will enable the Employer to pay the Contract Price... in accordance with Clause 14, Contract Price and Payment'*. The Employer is required to respond within 28 days of receiving the Contractor's request.

Should the Employer fail to respond, then Sub-Clause 16.1 entitles the Contractor (after 21 days' notice) to 'suspend the work or reduce the rate of work'. Termination under Sub-Clause 16.2 provides the ultimate remedy.

2.5   Employer's Claims

The Employer and the Contractor would most likely agree that any payments one to another for the supply of miscellaneous goods and services would be amicably arranged and payment made by commercial invoices independently of payments falling under the scope of Sub-Clause 14.7, Payment. However, circumstances may arise which entitle the Employer to claim payment from the Contractor under various Contract clauses which are identified and listed in Appendix D.

Sub-Clause 2.5 describes the procedure to be followed by the Employer should he consider himself to be entitled to payment from the Contractor under the terms of the Contract.

The Employer (or the Engineer on his behalf) is required to give notice of the Employer's claim with particulars as soon as practicable after the Employer becomes aware of the event or circumstances giving rise to the claim. The notice shall be given to the Engineer in writing and copied to the Contractor.

No notice is required for payments due to the Employer under:

- Sub-Clause 4.19, Electricity, Water, Gas
- Sub-Clause 4.20, Employer's Equipment and Free-issue Material
- Other services provided by the Employer to the Contractor.

The particulars of the claim shall specify the clause of the Contract entitling the Employer to make the claim and substantiate the amount which the Employer considers due under the Contract.

The procedure to be followed by the Employer in presenting claims is in its essentials similar to that to be followed by the Contractor in presenting his claims against the Employer under Clause 20.1, Contractor's Claims. The notable difference is that there are no time limits (unless required by applicable law) for the Employer to present his claims, in sharp contrast to the strict time limits applied to any Contractor's Claims.

(*Note*: The MDB Harmonised Pink Book has different requirements. The Employer is required to give notice *'as soon as practical and no longer than 28 days after... the event or circumstances giving rise to the claim'*.)

The FIDIC Contracts Guide states that the Employer's Claims are to be included in the monthly progress reports described in Sub-Clause 4.21,

Progress Reports. Considering that the progress reports are prepared by the Contractor, this requirement is likely to be neglected and requires enforcement.

Following receipt of a claim from the Employer, the Engineer is required to proceed in accordance with Sub-Clause 3.5, Determinations, to agree or determine the amount (if any) which the Employer is entitled to be paid by the Contractor. The relevant procedures are discussed further in Chapter 2 of this book.

The amount determined by the Engineer to be due to the Employer under Sub-Clause 3.5 can then be deducted by the Employer from Interim Payment Certificates.

Also within this Sub-Clause 2.5 FIDIC has chosen to deal with matters arising from claims arising from Sub-Clause 11.3, Extension of Defects Notification, entitling the Employer to claim an extension of the Defects Notification Period for the Works, Section or major item of Plant which after taking over cannot be used for their intended purpose by reason of a defect or fault falling under the Contractor's responsibility. Any claims made by the Employer under Sub-Clause 11.3 shall follow the procedures given in Sub-Clause 3.5.

Clause 3 The Engineer

The majority of the sub-clauses under this heading relate to the activities of the Engineer and are discussed in detail in Part 2. Only those sub-clauses identified below require the direct intervention of the Employer.

3.1 Engineer's Duties and Authority

The Employer is required to appoint the Engineer to carry out the duties assigned to him in the Contract. Ideally the Employer should identify the Engineer in the tender documents (Appendix to Tender) as this will permit the Contractor to make his own evaluation of the quality of the Engineer.

If the Engineer cannot be identified at the date of tender, it is important that the Engineer be appointed and be available to carry out his duties prior to the Contractor commencing the Works.

In preference to suspending the Works and incurring delays and standing costs, the Employer may be tempted to appoint one of his own staff as a temporary substitute for the Engineer if the Engineer is not yet appointed. This is a most unsatisfactory arrangement, as the Employer's staff member will not be perceived to have independence, particularly with respect to contractual issues and will likely provoke an adverse reaction from the Contractor, particular if an intended short period of substitution becomes extended. A short-term appointment of a substitute independent engineer with appropriate experience may prove a better if still unsatisfactory option.

The appointment of the Engineer (and in a timely fashion) is crucial to most FIDIC-based contracts and consequently the Employer is required to make every effort to ensure the Engineer is available to undertake his duties prior to the Contractor commencing with the Works.

3.4 Replacement of the Engineer

The Employer may necessarily have to replace the Engineer for a variety of reasons. He is required to give 42 days' notice to the Contractor of his intention to replace the Engineer, the intended date of replacement and particulars of the replacement.

Within this notice period of 42 days the Contractor has the right to object in writing to the appointment of the replacement and giving detailed particulars for objecting. It is possible that the proposed replacement and the Contractor have had an unhappy relationship in the past and the Contractor considers that the risk assumed in his tender has increased.

It is appropriate that the Employer and the Contractor discuss any replacement proposal at an early stage to avoid any potential conflict however small that possibility might be.

3.5 Determinations

Sub-Clauses 2.5 and 20.1 specify the procedures to be adopted by each Party for the submission of claims for financial compensation and/or extension of time in accordance with Sub-Clauses 11.3 and 8.4 respectively. Having received notice of claim and detailed particulars, the Engineer is required to proceed in accordance with Sub-Clause 3.5 and consult with each Party to agree or determine the extension of time or the amount of financial compensation due.

If agreement is not achieved, then the Engineer shall make a fair determination. The Engineer's determination is not required to be made impartially, unless there are specific provisions in the Particular Conditions. However, the Engineer shall act in a responsible, professional manner and where required, shall engage suitably qualified engineers and other professionals to assist him in his duties.

The FIDIC Contracts Guide states '*The Engineer does not proceed in accordance with Sub-Clause 3.5 only once in respect of each claim. He does so in stages as further particulars are submitted under Sub-Clause 20.1 until the extension and financial compensation are finally agreed or determined*'.

Sub-Clause 3.2, Delegation by the Engineer, prohibits the Engineer from delegating his authority to determine any matter which is to be determined in accordance with this Sub-Clause 3.5, unless agreed otherwise by the Parties.

Sub-Clause 1.3 requires that the Engineer's determination be given in writing to the Parties. The Engineer's Determination shall not be unduly delayed or withheld.

Clause 4 The Contractor

4.0 General

This clause describes the obligations and duties and other matters concerning the role of the Contractor and inevitably touches upon issues which are of direct concern to the Employer. Commentary is centred on those sub-clauses which directly involve the Employer.

Other issues which are related to the role of the Engineer are given in Chapter 2 of this book.

4.1 Contractor's General Obligations

This sub-clause describes in broad detail the general obligations of the Contractor.

The Contractor is required to:

- '*design (to the extent specified in the Contract), execute and complete the Works*'. The extent of the Contractor's involvement in design should be clearly expressed in the Contract Documents. Any lack of clarity should be queried in the Tender period. The Engineer is responsible for the coordination of designs
- provide all manpower, plant and materials, whether of permanent or temporary nature, required for the design, execution and completion of the Works, including remedying the defects
- take responsibility for adequacy, stability and safety of all Site operations. The Contractor is required to submit details of all arrangements (e.g. plant and office layouts) and methods of execution ('Method Statements')
- follow specified procedures for the submittal of Contractor's Documents for any part of the Permanent Works designed by the Contractor. Further, the Contractor is requested to submit 'as built' documents together with operation and maintenance manuals for those parts of the Works designed by him.

4.2 Performance Security

Within 28 days after receiving the Letter of Acceptance, the Contractor is required to submit the Performance Security to the Employer with a copy provided to the Engineer. The form of the Performance Security and the entity providing it are subject to the written approval of the Employer (and not the Engineer), although it may be assumed that the Engineer will provide the Employer with any assistance he may require. The Performance Security is to be kept in the safe custody of the Employer.

Example forms of the Performance Security are provided as annexures to the Red Book. Two types are offered, a demand guarantee type and a surety bond. The demand guarantee type is largely favoured by the Employer and the relevant model form will form part of the Contract Documents.

Importantly, the model form defines the expiry date as the *'expected expiry of the Defects Notification Period for the Works'*, although the Employer is entitled to present claims against the Performance Security for a further period of 70 days.

Not infrequently many smaller contractors find their guarantee providers (often their own bankers) limit the expiry date of the guarantee to the expected date of taking over. This non-compliance could be avoided if Employers were to specify that the proposed provider be identified in the tender together with a statement from the proposed provider, confirming that the guarantee will be fully compliant with the requirements of the Contract and not restrict the validity period of the guarantee.

Having awarded the Contract, the Employer will have the intention to allow the Contractor to commence the Works without undue delay, and may be faced with a difficult decision whether to allow the Contractor to proceed with a non-compliant guarantee or to have to deal with a major breach of Contract by the Contractor.

If, as is frequently the case, the Employer accepts the non-compliance, there is a real possibility that the validity period of the guarantee will later need extending. Should doubts exist concerning the ability of the Contractor to complete the Works, events may arise which make it difficult to get the validity period of the guarantee extended.

The Engineer will have a significant input in providing assistance to the Employer to resolve these issues, since he will be best placed to evaluate the period the guarantee is required to be extended.

4.3 Contractor's Representative

Unless the Contractor's Representative is named in the Contract, the Contractor is required to submit to the Engineer for consent the name and particulars of the person who he proposes to appoint as the Contractor's Representative.

There is no involvement of the Employer in this process, but it may be expected that he will wish to be involved in the approval procedure.

4.4 Subcontractors

The Contractor is not allowed to subcontract all of the Works. A limit to the amount which can be subcontracted is to be provided by the Employer in the Contract Documents. There is also a possibility that local subcontractors may be given preference in selected areas of work.

The Subcontractor is required to obtain the prior consent of the Engineer if he intends to subcontract parts of the Works with the proviso that no approval is required in respect of subcontractors named in the tender. Consequently, if the Employer (or the Engineer) has objection to a named subcontractor, then any objection has to be resolved in post-tender discussions and prior to the signing of the Contract Agreement.

4.5 Assignment of Benefit of Subcontract

In some circumstances the obligations of the Subcontractor may extend beyond the expiry date of the relevant Defects Notification Period. For example elevators, air conditioning units and similar may have to be maintained for a period well in excess of the defects notification period for which the Contractor is liable under the Contract.

Experienced Employers and Engineers are well aware of the need to retain the services of the Subcontractor after the departure of the Contractor from Site. For the most part subcontractors welcome the possibility of extended maintenance contracts (or material supply) and are willing to accept the assignment of the benefit of the subcontract to the Employer.

At the time of preparing his tender the Contractor should check if provisions have been included in the tender documents for the assignment of benefit of the subcontract to the Employer. If there is no such provision, then the Contractor should ask the Engineer to clarify the requirements of the Employer. In any event the issue of assignment has to be addressed in the subcontract documents.

4.6 Co-operation

It is preferable that the Employer ensures that the tender documents describe the extent of the co-operation to be provided by the Contractor in order that the Contractor may make appropriate allowance in his tender.

If the scope of co-operation is extended beyond that reasonably foreseeable at the time of tender, then any additional cost incurred by the Contractor shall be the subject of a variation.

4.7 Setting Out

The Employer is required to arrange for the primary setting out to be established by others. He now has the obligation to provide the setting out information to the Contractor either directly or via the Engineer. The handover is likely to require a site inspection of survey beacons to ensure that all exist and none are disturbed, in which case the Employer is liable for their reinstatement.

4.8 Safety Procedures

The Employer has no direct involvement in the establishment of safety procedures, excepting that his own personnel will be required to fully co-operate with the Contractor and the Engineer.

4.9 Quality Assurance

All matters relating to Quality Assurance are to be dealt with by the Contractor under the supervision of the Engineer. The Employer has no direct involvement.

4.10 Site Data

This sub-clause requires that the Employer makes available to the Contractor prior to the Base Date '*all relevant information in the Employer's possession of sub-surface and hydrological conditions at the Site including environmental aspects*'. The Employer may choose to supply this information as part of the Tender documentation or, if the data is bulky, he may invite tenderers to inspect the data at a given location.

The Contractor is responsible for his own interpretation of such data.

Other key data may be available from other sources, particularly government offices and agencies. This could include statistical data, indices, labour laws including levels of pay, company law and similar. The Contractor is solely responsible for identifying, collecting and analysing this data. It is a truism that a tenderer given unlimited time and unlimited resources could discover everything necessary for a risk-free project. This is clearly not a practical consideration for a tenderer preparing his offer in a limited period of time. FIDIC recognises this reality by stating that '*... to the extent which was practicable (taking into account of cost and time), the Contractor shall be deemed to have obtained all necessary information...*'.

This criterion of practicality has a profound influence on any claim the Contractor may wish to make under the provisions of Sub-Clause 4.12, Unforeseeable Physical Conditions. The Contractor's tender office would be well advised to keep copies or records of the data provided by the Employer, together with copies or records of data obtained elsewhere, which had an influence on his tender. These may be important in the evaluation of claims.

Under this sub-clause the '*Contractor is deemed to have inspected and examined the Site before submitting his Tender offer*'.

It is not an obligatory duty, but the majority of employers organise a formal inspection of the Site which the Contractor may be obliged to attend as a precondition of the tendering process. Should the Site be in a restricted area, the formal inspection may be the only opportunity for the Contractor to inspect the Site. It is recommended that the Contractor properly prepare himself for any site inspection. Clarifications should be sought, where appropriate, from the Employer/Engineer. A written record should be prepared complete with a photographic record for future reference.

Should the Employer come into possession of other data after the Base Date, he is obliged to supply the same to the tenderers (Contractor) for evaluation. It may be that the other Data may lead to claims for additional payment from the Contractor. However, if the Employer negligently or intentionally withholds data, he may leave himself exposed to legal action, especially in the event of death or injury or loss during the execution of the Works.

4.11 Sufficiency of the Accepted Contract Amount

'The Contractor is deemed to have satisfied himself as to the correctness and sufficiency of the Accepted Contract Amount and to have based the Accepted Contract Amount on the matters referred to in Sub-Clause 4.10 "Site Data".'

4.12 Unforeseeable Physical Conditions

Having provided Contract Data as required by Sub-Clause 4.10, the Employer has no formal duties in respect of any claim presented by the Contractor under the provisions of this sub-clause, but, as a consequence of being a central figure in the preparation of the Contract Documents, the Employer will have an important role in the evaluation of any claim made by the Contractor under the provisions of this sub-clause.

4.13 Rights of Way and Facilities

Sub-Clause 2.1, Right of Access to Site, requires that the Employer provides the Contractor with the right of access to Site. The Contractor has the obligation to prepare the access according to his needs. Should the Contractor require other rights of access to Site or other areas, which are not areas to be provided by the Employer, then the Contractor is obliged to make appropriate arrangements at his own risk and expense.

4.14 Avoidance of Interference

The Contractor shall not improperly cause any interference with the public, including access to and use of roads and footpaths, irrespective of ownership. The Contractor shall indemnify the Employer for all claims for damages resulting from any improper interference.

However, the FIDIC Contracts Guide qualifies this liability by referring to Sub-Clauses 17.1 and 18.3(d)(ii), wherein the Employer is required to indemnify the Contractor from 'damage which unavoidably arises of the Contractor's obligations'. However, damage which arises as a consequence of the Contractor's chosen methods of executing the Works is a Contractor's responsibility.

4.15 Access Route

The Employer is not responsible for any claims arising from the use by the Contractor of any access route, nor does the Employer guarantee the suitability of any particular access route.

It may happen that the local authorities may have objection to the use of a particular access by the Contractor, even though the access may be a public road. In such instances the Contractor may have a valid claim under Sub-Clause 2.2, Permits, licences or approvals, or under Sub-Clause 8.5, Delays caused by local Authorities. The assistance of the Employer to overcome access difficulties would clearly be of benefit to the progress of the Works.

4.16 Transport of Goods

On receiving notice of the anticipated arrival date on site of Plant or a major item of other Goods, the Employer and Engineer should consider if any action is required by them, e.g. inspection, storage arrangements, etc.

4.17 Contractor's Equipment

The Contractor's Equipment, when brought to Site, is deemed to be exclusively for use on the Works.

The consent of the Engineer is to be obtained before the Contractor is allowed to remove Contractor's Equipment from Site.

4.18 Protection of the Environment

The Employer will need to have satisfied all requirements of the appropriate authorities in respect of protection of the environment. This approval process is likely to have identified specific obligations and duties to be observed during the period of executing the Works. The Employer can be expected to include appropriate data in the Contract Documents and identify any specific obligations and duties of the Contractor.

These obligations and duties will be wide ranging from dust control in quarries to disposal of waste. The Contractor will be obliged to provide statements concerning his proposed method of fulfilling these obligations.

4.19 Electricity, Water and Gas

The Contractor is responsible for the provision of all power, water and other services he may require. He shall make his own provisions, either using his own resources or the services provided by external service providers, and shall include the cost of these services in his tender price.

It may happen that there are existing supplies of services on the Site, which are in the control or ownership of the Employer. The Employer may require the Contractor to make use of these existing services, particularly if he is the sole source of supply and there are a number of consumers (including other Contractors) on or near the Site.

The Employer shall provide the terms and conditions of these services to the Contractor together with pricing details. The Contractor shall include the cost in his tender price.

4.20 Employer's Equipment and Free-Issue Material

(a) The Employer may have available Employer's Equipment, which he can offer at stated prices to the Contractor for incorporation in the Works, thereby reducing the overall cost of the project. The Employer shall prepare and include in the tender documents full details of the availability, prices, specifications and any other key data.

(b) The Employer may have materials (the 'free-issue' materials), which can be used by the Contractor in the execution of the Works free of charge. Full details of these free issue materials shall be provided in the Specifications. The Contractor has to make his own decision whether or not to use these free-issue materials.

It is likely that tenderers would request to inspect both the Employer's Equipment and the free-issue materials in the pre-tender period.

The Bill of Quantities should contain bill items for the supply of all specified equipment and materials available with the Employer, and alternate bill items for the supply of the same items by the Contractor through his own purchasing office.

The sequencing of the hand-over of these items to the Contractor is discussed in Chapter 2, Sub-Clause 4.20 of this book.

4.21 Progress Reports

The Conditions of Contract do not require any involvement of the Employer in the preparation and presentation of Progress Reports.

4.22 Security of the Site

Although this sub-clause allocates primary responsibility for the security of the Site to the Contractor, there may be situations when it is more appropriate that the Employer assumes primary control and responsibility (e.g. security of a Site that is part of an existing operational facility).

Should the Contractor have responsibility for security, it will be necessary to define the scope of his responsibilities, including geographical limits. The Contractor will be expected to provide a detailed security plan for the consent of the Employer and the Engineer.

4.23 Contractor's Operations on Site

The Contractor has general obligations to confine his operations to the Site (and any additional areas) and to keep the Site free from obstructions, surplus materials and waste. No specific duties are allocated to the Employer in this regard, as the Engineer will be tasked with ensuring compliance.

4.24 Fossils

As the FIDIC Contracts Guide notes '.... *fossils and other antiquities are the property and also the liability of the Employer, although other parties may have rights and/or liabilities*'.

Should there be an expectation that fossils or antiquities would be encountered, it would be beneficial if a procedural plan was pre-arranged by the Employer to allow immediate action to be taken, thus minimising the possibility of a claim for delay from the Contractor.

Clause 5 Nominated Subcontractors

5.0 General

This clause of the Contract is prefaced in the FIDIC Contracts Guide with some notes of caution. Although these advisory notes are primarily directed towards the Employer and the Engineer, they are also of interest to Contractors as they provide an insight into the reasoning behind the engagement of nominated Subcontractors for the Works:

(i) *'If there are restrictions relating to the manufacture of certain items of Plant or Materials, the specification may refer to the named manufacturer without making him a nominated Subcontractor'*.
(ii) If the Employer requires that *a part of the Works 'is executed by a specialist company, the Specification may include a list of acceptable Subcontractors'* inviting the Contractor to make his own choice. *'The selected Subcontractor would not then be a nominated Subcontractor'*.
(iii) Should the Employer wish to become significantly involved in design and execution using a specialist company, a separate contract may be preferable.

The Conditions of Contract do not specifically identify which Party shall investigate enquiries for potential subcontractors and which Party shall be responsible for conducting negotiations with preferred subcontractors.

It is likely that the Employer, with the assistance of the Engineer, will have identified potential subcontractors and will provide them with appropriate documentation in order that they can provide tender offers.

Once the preferred subcontractor is identified, the Contractor will need to join in any discussions to ensure that the subcontracted Works are acceptably coordinated and contractual issues settled.

As a consequence of the above there is potentially a considerable benefit to both Parties should the Employer involve the Contractor at an early stage of his negotiations with prospective nominated Subcontractors in order that any additional requirements of the Subcontractors can be identified and quantified. In addition this consultative process would provide opportunity for discussion on technical issues and the programming of the subcontracted Works.

The Contractor does not have to accept any greater risk than the risk already contained within the Contract, particularly with respect to key issues such as insurances and payment conditions. Unless specifically stated in the Contract, the Contractor is under no obligation to provide other services such as vehicles, accommodation, materials, and use of Contractor services notably workshop services. The percentage for the Contractor's overheads and profit does not include the cost of these additional services, if available. It is preferable that the Subcontractor shall include these costs within his subcontract price and pay the Contractor for any consumption on an 'as and when' basis provided always that the Contractor is able and willing to provide those additional services.

Once all issues have been agreed between the Parties and the Subcontractor, then the subcontract document can be drawn up, and reviewed by the Engineer prior to signature by the Contractor and Subcontractor.

The nominated Subcontractor will be required to provide the Contractor with a Performance Security and evidence of his insurances. Should the nominated Subcontractor be the beneficiary of an Advance Payment, an Advance Payment Guarantee will be required. These and similar matters need to be addressed in the preparation of the subcontract documents for subcontracted Works.

5.1 Definition of 'Nominated Subcontractor'

'The term "nominated Subcontractor" means a Subcontractor:

(a) *who is stated in the Contract to be a nominated Subcontractor'*. In addition to technical information contained in the Contract, a Provisional Sum will have been included in the Bills of Quantities (cross-refer to Sub-Clause 13.5) or

(b) *'whom the Engineer instructs the Contractor to employ as a Subcontractor'*. For payment purposes such instruction shall be referenced to Sub-Clause 13.3 'Variations' or Sub-Clause 13.6 'Daywork'.

5.2 Objection to Nomination

The Contractor has the right to object to the engagement of a nominated Subcontractor. He is required to give notice of his objection to the Engineer as soon as practical with reasoning for his objection. Reasons for objection could include:

- concerns that the Subcontractor does not have the required expertise, experience, resources or financial strength
- failure of the Employer to agree to indemnify the Contractor against negligence by the nominated Subcontractor
- the subcontract does not specify that the nominated Subcontractor will undertake the obligations and liabilities in such a manner and timing as will *'enable the Contractor to fulfil his own obligations and liabilities under the Contract'*
- *'the subcontract does not indemnify the Contractor against and from all obligations and liabilities arising under the Contract and from the consequences of any failure by the Subcontractor to meet his obligations and liabilities arising under the subcontract.'*

5.3 Payments to Nominated Subcontractors

'The Contractor shall pay to the nominated Subcontractor the amounts which the Engineer certifies to be due in accordance with the subcontract'. The Contractor shall be paid the same amount plus a percentage for the Contractor's overheads and profit.

It is appropriate the subcontract document provides that the Contractor pays the Subcontractor within a fixed number of days from the date on which the Contractor receives corresponding payment under the Contract. The number of days is to be specifically stated in the subcontract documents.

5.4 Evidence of Payments

Before issuing a Payment Certificate which includes an amount payable to a nominated Subcontractor, the Engineer may request evidence that previously certified amounts due under the Subcontract have been paid to the Subcontractor.

The Employer will rightly also be concerned if there are late or under payments by the Contractor to the Subcontractor, not least because it may be an early sign of the financial instability of the Contractor.

Any failure by the Contractor to make payment to nominated Subcontractors when due may entitle the Employer to make direct payment.

Especially on very large projects it is recommended that matters concerning the Contract (which involve the Employer and the Engineer) are separated from those matters solely concerning the Contractor and the nominated Subcontractor. Any claims or disputes between Contractor and the nominated Subcontractor which directly relate to the performance of the Contract have to be managed to conform to the requirements of the Contract. Claims and disputes which solely relate to the contractual relationship between the Contractor and the nominated Subcontractor have to be managed in accordance with the Subcontract, where there is likely to be greater scope for flexibility without the involvement of the Employer and/or the Engineer.

Similarly, payments due to the Subcontractor under the terms of the Contract should preferably be managed separately from other domestic payment matters such as payment for any services provided. It is recommended that the Contractor ensures that formal interim payment certificates are issued to the nominated Subcontractor once the Contractor receives his own certification under the Contract. Any other payment due from the Contractor to the nominated Subcontractor or vice versa should be dealt with separately as a simple commercial transaction in order that the content of the Interim Payment Certificates is not obscured.

Clause 6 Staff and Labour

6.1 Engagement of Staff and Labour

The Contract does not require the Employer to become involved with the Contractor's arrangements for the recruitment of his labour force. However, the Contract may contain restrictions on the use of expatriate staff and labour.

6.2 Rates of Wages and Conditions of Labour

The Employer has no direct involvement in this subject but may request that he is kept informed of any developments which might affect the progress of the Works.

Not infrequently there are likely to be political and social issues which will affect the wages and conditions of labour. The Employer would be ideally placed to provide guidance to the Contractor, particularly if the Contractor is not experienced in local conditions and practices.

6.3 Persons in Service of Employer

The Contractor is prohibited from engaging staff or labour from amongst the Employer's personnel. However, it is possible that there may be provisions in the Contract for the Contractor to provide work experience to a limited number of the Employer's personnel. This experience training is separate to any formal training required under the provisions of Sub-Clause 5.5, Training.

6.4 Labour Laws

The Contractor is required to comply with the relevant labour laws and may require the assistance of the Employer in fulfilling all requirements which would enable him to recruit the staff and labour required to execute the Contract.

6.5 Working Hours

The Contractor is not permitted to work '...*on the site on locally recognised days of rest or outside the normal working hours stated in the Appendix to Tender unless:*

(a) *otherwise stated in the Contract*
(b) *the Engineer gives consent*
(c) *the work is unavoidable or necessary for the protection of life or property...*'

It often happens that the work hours given in the Appendix to Tender reflect the Employer's own work practice (particularly if he is a state-controlled body) and by extension the work hours to be worked by the Engineer whose costs are also met by the Employer.

Although the Engineer may be willing to give the Contractor consent to work additional hours, he may be constrained from doing so because he has no agreement in place that would remunerate him for the additional costs of his own supervisory staff. Suggestions that the Contractor should reimburse these additional engineering costs directly to the Engineer are not appropriate, as such arrangement would be liable to abuse.

In the preparation of the tender documents the Employer should give consideration to the nature of the work necessarily required in the execution of the Works and the consequential effect on the working hours likely to be worked by a successful contractor.

Considerations typically include:

- operations for which multi-shift working is required
- operations affected by season. Asphalting may not be possible or permitted in cold (winter) months, but extended hours could be worked in long warmer summer months
- concreting operations could be restricted to daylight hours, but subsidiary activities including form stripping, curing operations, etc. could take place at night
- maintenance and other operations including the transportation of materials, which require minimal supervision by the Engineer, could also take place at night.

The working hours finally included in the Appendix to Tender have an important consequence in the programming and execution of the Works, which will be reflected in the valuation of tenders offered. A contractor preparing his tender is obliged to comply with the stated working hours.

6.7 Health and Safety

The Employer's Personnel are required to co-operate with the Contractor in the execution of his duties under this sub-clause.

The extent (if any) that the Contractor is required to provide medical services to the Employer's Personnel on Site in excess of first aid should be clearly stated.

6.8 Contractor's Superintendence

There is no specific involvement of the Employer.

6.9 Contractor's Personnel

In the event of unacceptable behaviour by a member of the Contractor's work force, the Employer is likely to instruct the Engineer to order the removal of the offender from site, not withstanding that this sub-clause does not specifically entitle him to do so directly.

6.10 Records of Contractor's Personnel and Equipment

There is no specific involvement of the Employer.

6.11 Disorderly Conduct

This sub-clause refers to '*disorderly conduct*' by the Contractor's Personnel. The primary responsibility to '*preserve peace and protection of persons and property*' lies with the Contractor. The Employer would wish to be kept informed of occurrences which fall under this heading.

Clause 7 Plant, Materials and Workmanship

The majority of sub-clauses under this heading relate to the activities of the Engineer and are discussed in detail in Chapter 2. Only those sub-clauses identified below require the direct involvement of the Employer.

7.3 Inspection

It may be necessary for the Engineer and/or the Employer to inspect the progress of Plant under manufacture off-site. If the place of manufacture is in another country, the Employer will need to prepare a plan for how the inspection will be managed. Unless specifically stated otherwise in the Contract, the Contractor is not responsible for any costs incurred by the Engineer or the Engineer attending the inspection.

7.7 Ownership of Plant and Materials

'*Each item of Plant and Materials shall........... become the property of the Employer.... free from liens....*

(a) *when it is delivered to site*
(b) *when the Contractor is entitled to payment of the value of the Plant and Materials in Event of Suspension*'.

Both 'Plant' and 'Materials' are defined in part as 'Intended to form part of the Permanent Works', Sub-Clauses 1.1.5.3 and 1.5.5.5 refer. Each item of Plant and Materials becomes the property of the Employer when it is delivered to site.

In contrast all Contractor's Goods (Sub-Clause 1.1.5.2), which includes Contractor's Equipment, Materials, Plant and Temporary Works, do not become the property of the Employer under the terms of the Contract.

The FIDIC Contracts Guide provides a warning '*As a legal matter, it may be important to establish the ownership of Plant and Materials, particularly in case of bankruptcy/liquidation of the person who is in possession of them*'. And further '*The owner of the goods may be liable for the payment of taxes and duties, and ownership may also be a factor in determining liability for care, custody and control*'.

Supply subcontracts are required to be consistent with the Contract. Any inconsistency may cause difficulties with the supply contractors attempting to recover goods already supplied if there is a failure by the Contractor.

Attention is also drawn to Sub-Clause 15.2, Termination by the Employer, which in part requires the Contractor on Termination to deliver '*any required Goods... to the Engineer*'. Legal advice should be obtained in the event of any primary failure by the Contractor and before there is any attempt to remove any of the Contractor's Goods from Site.

Clause 8 Commencement, Delays and Suspension

A number of sub-clauses under this heading relate to the activities of the Engineer and are discussed in detail in Chapter 2. Only the sub-clauses identified below require the direct involvement of the Employer.

8.1 Commencement of Work

The Engineer is required to give the Contractor 7 days' notice of the Commencement Date and will require the corresponding authority of the Employer to do so. The Commencement Date shall be not later than 42 days after the Contractor receives the Letter of Acceptance from the Employer. Thereafter the Contractor shall commence work as soon as reasonably practical.

If there is no Letter of Acceptance, Sub-Clause 1.1.1.3 states the expression 'Letter of Acceptance means the Contract Agreement and the date of issuing the Letter of Acceptance means the date of signing the Contract Agreement'. If the Contract Agreement specifies a Commencement Date, it is binding.

8.2 Time for Completion

It is the Contractor's fundamental time-related obligation to complete within the Time for Completion. The Time for Completion can only be extended in accordance with the procedures given in Sub-Clause 8.4, Extension of Time for Completion.

8.4 Extension of Time

This Sub-Clause identifies the circumstances which would entitle the Contractor to claim an Extension of Time for Completion. Most likely a successful claim will be accompanied by the presentation of a further claim for additional payment. The Employer and the Engineer will need to prepare an efficient strategy for administering such claims.

8.5 Delay Caused by Authorities

Public authorities frequently have difficulties in dealing expeditiously with the requests and requirements of the Contractor, even if the Contractor has adhered to the procedures laid down by the authorities. Frequently delays arise because the authority is under-resourced to cope with the additional workload arising from the Contractor's requirements. Additional complications occur invariably if more than one public authority is involved.

Provided that the Contractor has diligently followed the required procedures, the Contractor is entitled to claim both an extension of time and to additional compensation.

The Employer, particularly if he is also a state organisation, may be able to help resolve problems before they become critical, possibly by requesting practical assistance from the Contractor. This can be expected to be more cost effective than allowing delays to the Works.

8.6   Rate of Progress

Should the progress of the Works fall behind the current programme under Sub-Clause 8.3, Programme, essentially for reasons within the Contractor's responsibility, then the Engineer can instruct the Contractor to submit proposals which will expedite progress and complete within the Time for Completion.

If the proposals of the Contractor cause the Employer to incur additional costs (in addition to Delay Damages Clause 8.7 refers) then, subject to Sub-Clause 2.5, the Contractor shall pay the Employer these additional costs.

8.7   Delay Damages

'If the Contractor fails to comply with Sub-Clause 8.2 "Time for Completion", the Contractor shall pay Delay Damages to the Employer for this default. The amount and limit for Delay Damages shall be as stated in the Appendix to Tender'.

'These Delay Damages shall be the only damages due from the Contractor as a consequence of the default (excepting in the event of Termination by the Employer Sub-Clause 15.2 '. The Employer cannot claim his actual costs, but equally does not have to demonstrate his actual loss.

The FIDIC Contracts Guide explains that *'the Contractor cannot prevent the imposition of Delay Damages by submitting claims for extension of time. However, the Employer may lose his entitlement to claim delay damages if he prevents extensions of time being agreed or determined in accordance with Sub-Clause 20.1'* (cross-refer to possible restrictions placed on the authority of the Engineer Sub-Clause 3.1).

Should he wish to claim Delay Damages, the Employer is required to present a documented claim to the Engineer, as provided for in Sub-Clause 2.5. The Engineer is required to formally review the claim in accordance with the provisions of Sub-Clause 3.5. It should be noted that Sub-Clause 3.5 requires the Engineer to consult with each Party before making a 'fair determination'. This procedure would give the Contractor the possibility to object should the Engineer be prevented by the Employer from making a determination in respect of the Contractor's existing claims for extensions of time.

8.8 Suspension of the Works

A situation may arise which necessitates the Engineer instructing the Contractor to suspend the execution of the Works and to protect the Works against deterioration, loss or damage. The Engineer shall state the reasons for the suspension.

The Contractor is not entitled to an extension of time for any delay or payment of costs:

- if the suspension is due to a cause attributable to the Contractor
- if the delay or costs arise from a Contractor's faulty design, workmanship or materials
- if the delay or costs arise from a failure of the Contractor to protect (or store) the Works against deterioration.

If the reason for the suspension arises from a Contractor's risk event, then the provisions of the following Sub-Clauses 8.9, 8.10 and 8.11 do not apply.

8.9 Consequences of Suspension

Subject to compliance with the procedures given in Sub-Clause 20.1, the Contractor shall be entitled to an extension of time corresponding to the period of suspension, with due allowance for the time required to resume the Works, together with payment of costs incurred as a consequence of delay. Clearly it is mutually beneficial if the Engineer and Contractor agree to maintain detailed records of the consequences of suspension.

8.10 Payment for Plant and Materials in Event of Suspension

The Contractor is entitled to the payment of the value of Plant and/or Materials which have not been delivered to Site if:

(a) *'the work on Plant and/or Materials have been suspended for more than 28 days and*
(b) *the Plant and/or Materials have been marked as Employer's property as instructed by the Engineer.'*

It may happen that the manufacture of Plant and Materials cannot be immediately suspended or that it would be a more economical option to complete the manufacture rather than suspend the work.

8.11 Prolonged Suspension

Should the suspension under Sub-Clause 8.8 continue for a period exceeding 84 days, the Contractor may request permission to restart work. If the Engineer does not give permission to start within a further period of 28 days, the Contractor has the option to give notice to the Engineer and treat the suspension as an omission of the affected part of the Works (refer to Sub-Clause 13, Variations and Omission). If the suspension affects the whole of the Works, the Contractor may give notice of termination under Sub-Clause 16.2, Termination by Contractor.

Prolonged suspension will give the Contractor considerable difficulties, particularly if the period of suspension cannot be predicted with reasonable certainty. For example, a decision may have to be taken to release workers or to send them on leave. Many of them may not return. A further consideration concerns the period of cover provided by the Contractor's export credit guarantee insurance, which may be severely restricted in the event of a prolonged suspension.

8.12 Resumption of Work

Once the Engineer grants permission to the Contractor to restart work, the Engineer and Contractor are required to jointly examine the Works and Plant and Materials affected by the suspension. A detailed report is appropriate, since the project insurances may be activated. The Contractor is obligated to make good any deterioration or loss, the cost of which will ultimately be to the account of the Employer or the subject of an insurance claim.

Clause 9 Tests on Completion

9.1 Contractor's Obligations

As an integral part of the Tests on Completion procedures, the Contractor is required to provide all documents described in Sub-Clause 4.1(d), Contractor's General Obligations. The preparation of these documents in an as-built condition may be a lengthy process and these will be subject to review by the Engineer.

The Contractor is to give the Engineer 21 days' notice of the date after which the Contractor will be ready to carry out each of the Tests on Completion which shall be carried out within 14 days of this date.

The Contractor is to provide the Engineer with a certified report of the Tests on Completion.

9.2 Delayed Tests

If the Tests on Completion are delayed by the Employer, Sub-Clauses 7.4 and 10.3 give the Contractor an entitlement to claim an extension of time and additional costs.

If the Tests on Completion are delayed by the Contractor, then the Engineer may give 21 days' notice requiring the Contractor to perform the tests. Thereafter the Employer's Personnel may proceed at the risk and cost of the Contractor. It must be considered if the Contractor is delaying the tests because the work is not complete and will not pass the Tests on Completion.

9.3 Re-testing

If the Works (or Section) fail to pass the Tests on Completion, the Engineer may require the tests to be repeated under the same terms and conditions.

9.4 Failure to Pass Tests on Completion

In the event of continued failure to satisfactorily complete the Tests on Completion, the Engineer may order further repeat testing (assumed to take place after checking and remedial work by the Contractor). If the continued failure to complete the Tests on Completion prevails, the Employer has available the remedies provided for in Sub-Clause 11.4(c). Alternatively, the Employer may authorise the Engineer to issue the Taking-Over Certificate, which carries the implication that the reasons for the failure to satisfactorily complete the Tests on Completion do not damage the Employer's interests.

Clause 10 Employer's Taking Over

10.1 Taking Over of the Works and Sections

The Employer is obligated to take over the Works (or Section of the Works) once they have been completed by the Contractor and a Taking-Over Certificate issued by the Engineer. A Section is defined in Sub-Clause 1.1.5.6 as *'a part of the Works specified in the Appendix to Tender as a Section'*.

Once all work stated in the Contract is complete, excluding any minor outstanding work not materially affecting the Employer's use of the Works or Section, then the Contractor may make a written application to the Engineer for a Taking-Over Certificate to be issued.

The Employer should be wary of occupying the Works (or Section or Part of the Works) without following the given taking-over procedure since unilateral occupation is likely to be interpreted as an act of taking over.

Contrary to the procedures governing the Employer's taking over described in this sub-clause, differing practices apply in a number of countries. For example, in a number of former socialist countries in Eastern Europe the taking-over procedure is governed by local law which is likely to over-rule the standard FIDIC procedure. In these countries the taking-over procedure is conducted by a committee (and not by the Engineer) who have the duty not only to supervise the actual taking-over process, but also to confirm that the Works have been constructed in accordance with the technical standards specified in the Contract. The Employer will necessarily need to take a leading role in the provision of information to this committee.

10.2 Taking Over of Parts of the Works

Circumstances may arise where the Employer will consider taking over of a part of the Works which is not otherwise identified as a Section of the Works in the Appendix to the Tender.

It is likely that the Employer will only consider taking over a part of the Works where the part has value or usefulness to the Employer.

The Contractor has no contractual right to insist that the Employer takes over a part of the Works unless exceptionally the Employer has occupied that part. The Engineer cannot issue a Taking-Over Certificate for a part of the Works unless authorised to do so by the Employer.

The issue of a Taking-Over Certificate for a part of the Works requires an adjustment of the Delay Damages for the Works (or Section of the Works incorporating the part handed over). The Delay Damages shall be proportionately reduced according to the proportion that the value of the part taken over has to the value of the Works (or Section of the Works incorporating the part handed over).

The Employer is to be aware that the Contractor has an entitlement to payment in respect of additional costs incurred as a consequence of the Employer requiring the use and/or the taking over of a part of the Works unless such use is specified in the Contract.

10.3 Interference with Tests on Completion

Tests on Completion are the tests which are required to determine whether the Works (or a Section, if any) have reached the stage at which the Employer should take over the Works or Section. (Refer to Sub-Clause 9.1.)

Should the Employer prevent the Contractor from carrying out the Tests on Completion for a period exceeding 14 days, the Employer is deemed to have taken over the Works or Section on the date when the Taking-Over Certificate would otherwise have been completed. Should the Contractor suffer delay and/or incur additional costs, he is entitled to give notice of claim in accordance with the procedures given in Sub-Clause 20.1.

Clause 11 Defects Liability

11.1 Completion of Outstanding Work and Remedying Defects

The Contractor is obliged to complete any outstanding work stated in a Taking-Over Certificate. In addition, the Contractor is required to remedy defects and damage (which fall under his contractual responsibility) which may be notified by (or on behalf of) the Employer on or before the expiry date of the Defects Notification Period.

The Contractor does not have responsibility to provide for the rectification of defects and damage caused by the Employer as a consequence of his use of the Works, although the Contractor may be willing to assist for additional payment.

11.2 Cost of Remedying Defects

The Contractor is responsible for the cost and remedying defects and damage which fall under his contractual responsibility, whereas the Employer is responsible for the cost of remedying defects and damage not the responsibility of the Contractor.

Should the Contractor be required to remedy defects and damage which he considers fall under the Employer's responsibility, then he is required to carry out the work and give notice under Sub-Clause 20.1. If there is agreement that the Employer will pay the Contractor's costs, then Sub-Clause 13.3, Variation Procedure, shall apply.

11.3 Extension of Defects Notification Period

Should the Employer be unable to use the Works or Section or a major item of Plant for their intended purpose as a consequence of defects falling under the Contractor's responsibility, then, subject to the giving notice under Sub-Clause 2.5, Employer's Claims, the Employer is entitled to an extension of the Defects Notification Period of equal duration to the period of non-availability.

The Defects Notification Period shall not be extended by more than two years. Other limitations apply in the event of Suspension of the Works.

11.4 Failure to Remedy Defects

If the Contractor fails to remedy any defect or damage within a reasonable time fixed by the Employer, then the Employer has three options:

(a) to carry out the work himself (or by others) at the Contractor's cost. Subject to the requirements of Sub-Clause 2.5, Employer's Claims, the Contractor shall pay to the Employer his costs incurred in carrying out the work, or

(b) require the Engineer to agree to determine a reduction in the Contract Price in accordance with Sub-Clause 3.5, Determinations, or

(c) if the defect or damage is so serious that the item cannot be put to its intended use, then the Employer shall be entitled to recover all sums paid for the Works or parts thereof plus financing costs, dismantling costs, clearance costs and the cost of returning the defective items to the Contractor.

11.5 Removal of Defective Work

It may happen that a defective or damaged item of Plant has to be removed from Site for the purposes of investigation and repair. The Employer's consent in writing has to be obtained by the Contractor and the consent document should identify any specific conditions governing the removal from Site.

The Employer should consider whether it is appropriate to request a financial security in the form of a bank guarantee or equal.

11.9 Performance Certificate

'*Performance of the Contractor's obligations shall not be considered to have been completed until the Engineer has issued the Performance Certificate to the Contractor…*' and '*Only the Performance Certificate shall be deemed to constitute acceptance of the Works*'.

In consideration of the importance of the Performance Certificate, which signifies that the Contractor has completed his obligations under the Contract and that the Works are accepted, it is evident that the issue of the Performance Certificate will be subject to a joint prior review by the Employer and the Engineer before it is issued.

11.10 Unfulfilled Obligations

After the Performance Certificate has been issued, both the Employer and the Contractor are obliged to fulfil any obligations outstanding at that time. These obligations will include the settlement of all financial issues, including outstanding claims.

11.11 Clearance of Site

The Contractor is obliged to clear the Site of all remaining Contractor's Equipment, Temporary Works and site debris within 28 days of receipt of the Performance Certificate.

It can be anticipated that the Contractor will already have removed the bulk of his property from the Site prior to the issue of the Performance

Certificate. The Employer may decide to allow the Contractor to leave some items on site, with or without an additional payment. Otherwise the Employer is entitled to clear the Site and sell or otherwise dispose of all remaining items and restore the Site, all at the Contractor's expense. Any surplus funds shall be paid to the Contractor by the Employer.

Clause 12 Measurement and Evaluation

12.1 **Works to be Measured**

12.2 **Method of Measurement**

12.3 **Evaluation**

12.4 **Omissions**

The Employer is not required to be involved in the process of Measurement and Evaluation. However, he should be aware of the provisions of Sub-Clause 12.3 which provides rules governing the evaluation of new rates and prices (where there is no rate specified in the Contract for similar work) and for the valuation of works instructed under Clause 13, Variations and Adjustments.

The Employer may consider specifying the use of a published method of measurement, such as the Standard Method of Measurement, published by the Institution of Civil Engineers, London. Local methods of measurement may also be available.

Clause 13 Variations and Adjustments

13.0 General

As the FIDIC Contracts Guide acknowledges, '... *Variations are the source of many disputes*'.

The clauses of the Conditions of Contract dealing with Variations and Adjustments are written in a manner which in theory requires minimal input from the Employer. In general it is the duty of the Engineer to instruct and evaluate Variations with the necessary involvement of the Contractor. However, for a number of reasons noted elsewhere, the Employer is now frequently deeply involved in the processing of Variations and Adjustments. The reasons for this greater involvement are complex, but the dominant factor is that Employers in general, and public authorities in particular, are increasingly required rigorously to ensure that all expenditure is strictly controlled and budgets are not exceeded without full justification.

As a consequence, the Particular Conditions of Contract frequently contain supplementary provisions which prevent the Engineer from authorising variations without the prior authority of the Employer.

Employers generally and public authorities in particular will have mandatory internal procedures before additional payments can be made and to ensure that appropriate funding is available in respect of additional expenditure. As a consequence there can be a significant interval between the date when the need for a Variation is recognised and the date when the Engineer is finally authorised to process the Variation.

The Contractor may be reluctant to commence or continue with varied or additional work, the subject of the Variation, without assurance of payment which the Employer may not always be able to immediately provide.

In such circumstances there is a real risk that there will be delays to the execution of the Contract and an expectation that the Contractor is likely to submit claims consequent upon delay and disruption.

Consequently, should the Employer require that he is to be deeply involved in the administration of Variations and Adjustments, it is required that he has an administrative organisation that can deal with Variations and Adjustments in a most expeditious manner. The Engineer and his staff are necessarily a key part of that organisation.

Because of the requirement for strict control of expenditure, the practice of 'on account' payments to contractors is now neglected (and may be prohibited in some jurisdictions). 'On account' payments have the advantage of effectively confirming that the Variation was being processed and, importantly, provide the Contractor with interim funding, thereby reducing the likelihood that the Contractor will notify financial claims and/or request an extension of Time for Completion.

13.1 Right to Vary

This sub-clause states '*Variations may be initiated at any time prior to issuing the Taking-Over Certificate for the Works, either by an instruction or by a request for the Contractor to submit a proposal*'.

Although not so stated in the wording of this clause, there is another major issue experienced with many contracts which arises as a consequence of errors and omissions in the original design presented to the Contractor for construction purposes.

The designer of the Works is frequently directly engaged by the Employer under an individual design contract distinct from the engineering contract for the supervision of the construction of the Works. In many instances the Employer will have specified that the design will not only be suitable for tender purposes, but also for construction purposes. This philosophy is particularly true of many smaller infrastructure projects executed with strictly controlled funding provided by international financing organisations.

In some jurisdictions the description 'designer' describes suitable qualified persons, who are legally registered and approved to practice as designers. They are legally authorised to prepare and, if necessary, to amend designs. The FIDIC engineer has no authority to interfere in this process and act himself as a 'designer', unless he is legally registered to do so.

Problems will arise during the construction stage, if the design is found to be in error or otherwise requires amendment. The designer may not be readily available and may not have a contractual responsibility for amending his design. The Engineer supervising the construction is unlikely to have responsibility (contractually and/or legally) for materially amending the design produced by another engineer. Quite unexpectedly the Employer may be faced with having to not only arrange for a design change, but also to expeditiously arrange the documentation for a formal Variation to be compiled, internally approved and issued to the Contractor. There is the inevitable risk that the project may be delayed and the Contractor will submit claims for both additional payment and an extension of the Time for Completion.

Therefore it would be prudent for the Employer to have in place procedures (including provision for the participation of the designer), so that events as described above can be dealt with expeditiously.

Throughout this process of identifying and authorising of Variations and Adjustments it is pertinent to draw attention to the last paragraph of this sub-clause, which states '*The Contractor shall not make any alteration and/ or modification of the Permanent Works, unless and until the Engineer instructs or approves a Variation*'.

Should the Employer elect to control the variation procedure, it is important that he has an organisation that is able to proceed expeditiously if delays of the Works are to be avoided.

13.4 Payment in Applicable Currencies

Prior to the issue of tenders, the Employer will have decided the principles that are to be adopted in the calculation of the amounts of foreign currency to be paid to the Contractor.

There are a number of possible variations, but the standard approach is for all payments due to the Contractor to be valued entirely in local currency with a fixed portion to be paid in foreign currency at a fixed exchange rate. The portion to be paid in foreign exchange is invariably selected by the

Contractor and is intended to reflect the anticipated amount of foreign expenditure included in his tender price.

There are a number of potential exceptions to the general rule described above, including:

- payment for some elements of varied works, particularly where their price evaluation is not based on existing bill items (Sub-Clause 13.1)
- payment derived from the process of Value Engineering (Sub-Clause 13.2)
- payments to Nominated Subcontractors (Sub-Clause 5.3)
- payments in respect of Provisional Sums (Sub-Clause 13.5)
- payments for dayworks (Sub-Clause 13.6).

13.5   Provisional Sums

'Provisional Sum' is defined in Sub-Clause 1.1.4.10 as '… *a sum (if any) which is specified in the Contract as a provisional sum, for the execution of any part of the Works or for the supply of Plant, Materials or services under Sub-Clause 13.5…*'.

The inclusion of Provisional Sums in the Bill of Quantities identifies parts of the Works which are not required to be priced at the risk of the Contractor. The FIDIC Contracts Guide emphasises that '*It is important to define the scope of each Provisional Sum, because the scope will be excluded from the other elements of the Contract Price*'.

The FIDIC Contracts Guide further points out that this sub-clause opens with the wording '*Each Provisional Sum shall only be used, in whole or part…*', which means that the valuation of a Provisional Sum cannot be in excess of the amount provided in the Contract.

'*The Engineer or the Employer cannot increase the amount of a Provisional Sum by Variation or otherwise*'. Then rather ambiguously the FIDIC Contracts Guide states '… *if the amount stated in a Provisional Sum is exceeded, the Contractor must comply with the Engineer's instructions… but he may not be bound by the financial consequences… in respect of the excess*'.

Without further explanation on the matter of 'excess' the FIDIC Contracts Guide concludes '… *the amount to be included in each Provisional Sum should include a realistic estimate of the final amount which is anticipated to be used*'.

The FIDIC Red Book does not make any provision for the Employer or Engineer to introduce additional Provisional Sums once the Contract is finalised. Should a need arise for additional work with the characteristics of a Provisional Sum, it will be dealt with as a Variation as described elsewhere in this Clause 13 and consequently may be subject to different price arrangements.

In addition to reimbursement of the actual amounts expended in complying with the requirements of Provisional Sums, the Contractor is to be paid '*a sum of overhead charges and profit, calculated as a percentage of the actual amounts…*'.

This percentage sum is pre-determined by the Employer and is given in the tender documents in a Schedule of Provisional Sums (if any) or more conventionally in the Appendix to Tender. Should the Employer fail to ensure that a percentage sum is included somewhere in the tender, he may anticipate an adverse reaction from the Contractor if it is later asserted that the absence of an appropriate percentage sum is to be interpreted as 'nil'.

13.6 Daywork

Dayworks are intended to be limited to minor or incidental work which cannot be conveniently valued by any other means.

In arranging the preparation of the tender documents, the Employer has two basic choices:

- He may decide that the Contractor shall provide his own priced listing of standard daywork items. A variation is that the Employer provides a standard listing which the Contractor is required to price. The disadvantage of this method is that it is very difficult for the Employer to compare the unit prices offered by tenderers, nor yet to evaluate the net effect on the tender prices.
- A more sophisticated approach is for the Employer to include, as part of the tender documents, his own fully pre-priced listing of daywork items and require each tenderer to provide a percentage adjustment on a notional value of the total amount likely to be expended on dayworks. This method has the advantage that it permits the Employer to not only compare daywork rates, but also to evaluate the net effect on tender prices.

13.7 Adjustments for Changes in Legislation

This sub-clause provides for adjustments of the Contract Price to take account of any increase or decrease in cost arising either from a change in the Laws of the Country or from a change in the interpretation of existing laws, which affect the Contractor's performance of the Contract. Typically there may be statutory increases in the cost of fuels, labour rates and other items where the price of the resource is controlled by the Government.

Occasionally a change in legislation may cause delays to the Works.

The Contractor is required to give formal notice (as required by Sub-Clause 20.1) of his entitlement to claim both reimbursement of his additional costs and an extension of time.

13.8 Adjustment for Changes in Cost

This sub-clause provides formulae to adjust the contract values to reflect escalation of costs due to inflation.

In the preparation of tender documents the Employer is required to decide if the amounts payable to the Contractor shall be adjusted for rises or falls in the cost of labour, goods and other inputs required for the execution of the Works. For contracts with a short duration (typically of one year or less duration) it is unlikely that there will be provision for adjustment for changes in Cost, on the assumption that it is reasonable that the Contractor will be able to predict changes in Cost over short periods with reasonable accuracy.

For longer periods predictions for changes in Cost become increasingly speculative and this uncertainty will be reflected in higher tender prices. The assumption of this risk by the Employer will not only reduce tender prices, but will also enable tenderers to offer tender prices of greater certainty and accuracy.

Adjustments for changes in Cost in its most simple form could take the form of evaluating those changes in Cost by comparing the cost shown on the supplier invoices with the base cost on which the tender price is based. This may have applicability in a country where the adjustment is restricted to a limited number of items and where the means of production and pricing are controlled by the State, but it is unsuitable in a situation where there is a large content of foreign labour, goods and services incorporated in the Contract Price.

FIDIC has elected to use a method based on the use of formulae to calculate the adjustments for changes in Cost.

The amounts to be paid to the Contractor under this sub-clause are adjusted for rises or falls in the various inputs required for the performance of the Works. These amounts are evaluated by the addition or deduction of the amounts determined from the comparison of index values included in the formulae given in the sub-clause.

The Employer is to decide which resources shall be subject to the provisions of this sub-clause and the relative value of the factors to be used, only requiring tenderers to identify which indices best relate to his anticipated sourcing of the specified resources.

Alternatively the Employer may permit tenderers to identify their own factors and which indices shall be used, again because this selection relates to the tenderers' anticipated sourcing of specified resources.

The Employer should be aware that the division between local and foreign indices will proportionately determine the amounts of foreign currencies requiring financing.

It is possible that the event giving rise to an adjustment of the contract price could be attributed to either Sub-Clause 13.7 or Sub-Clause 13.8, but payment is only due once.

Clause 14 Contract Price and Payment

14.1 The Contract Price

This sub-clause describes how the Contract Price is to be defined and evaluated. There are no special duties allocated to the Employer, although it is recommended that the Employer familiarises himself with the fundamental principles described herein.

14.2 Advance Payment

The Employer undertakes to provide the Contractor with an interest-free loan for mobilisation. The total advance payment (usually 10% of the Contract Price) is to be stated in the Appendix to the Tender. If there is no provision for an Advance Payment provided in the Appendix to the Tender, then it signifies that no Advance Payment will be made.

The Contractor shall provide the Employer with a guarantee issued by an entity (usually a first class bank) in the country where the project is to be executed. It is recommended that, subject to a review of the requirements of the local law, the Employer specifies the use of FIDICs own standard form of the Advance Payment Security (Annex H in the standard Conditions of Contract for Construction – the 'Red Book').

This sub-clause specifies that the Advance Payment Guarantee is to remain valid until the advance payment has been repaid, but its amount may be progressively reduced by the amount repaid. The Employer should be wary of non-standard guarantees, particularly those which have a fixed expiry date (usually corresponding to the Time for Completion, Sub-Clause 8.2). There may be later difficulties in obtaining an extension to the advance payment guarantee, should the Contractor not be in good financial health.

The Employer (not the Engineer) is responsible for approving or otherwise rejecting the offered Advance Payment Guarantee and must keep the Engineer informed of developments, since the Engineer cannot action any application for an Interim Progress Payment containing Advance Payment until the Advance Payment Guarantee is provided and approved.

There have been a number of instances where unscrupulous contractors have offered bogus documentation purporting to be an Advance Payment Guarantee. Unless the Contractor is of the highest reputation or otherwise well known to the Employer, it is recommended that the Employer cross-checks with the provider bank that the documentation offered by the Contractor is genuine and registered in the appropriate bank registry.

It is also recommended that the Employer periodically requests documentary evidence demonstrating that the Advance Payment has been used for its stated purpose, namely to finance the Contractor's mobilisation costs and has not been improperly diverted for other purposes.

Sub-Clause 14.2 provides a standard method and timetable for the repayment of the advance payment. The standard method provides maximum benefit to the Contractor at the commencement of the contract when mobilisation is under way and yet ensures that the Advance Payment is completely repaid prior to the issue of the Taking-Over Certificate.

Once an Interim Payment Certificate has been issued, it is appropriate that the Employer informs the provider of the Advance Payment Guarantee in writing of the amount of the Advance Payment repaid by the Contractor.

14.3 Application for Interim Payment Certificates

The form of the Statement to be prepared and used by the Contractor requires the approval of the Engineer and although not so stated, will also need to meet the requirements of the Employer. The FIDIC Red Book requires the Contractor to submit the Statement at the end of each month. Should the Employer require that the Statements be submitted at other intervals, this has to be stated in the tender documents. The Issue of Interim Payment Certificates is the subject of Sub-Clause 14.6.

It is not required to include the Advance Payment in an Interim Payment Certificate, since such payment is subject to special payment conditions (refer to Sub-Clause 14.7). The Employer should consider if a separate Payment Certificate would satisfy his administrative requirements.

14.4 Schedule of Payments

This sub-clause describes the procedures to be followed when payments to the Contractor are to be evaluated by reference to a schedule of payments instead of a measurement process as described in Sub-Clause 14.3.

No specific duties or responsibilities are allocated to the Employer.

14.5 Plant and Materials Intended for the Works

This sub-clause entitles the Contractor to claim for a further interim advance payment in respect of Plant and Materials which have been sent to Site for incorporation in the Works. Sub-Clause 14.5 describes the terms and conditions governing any request made by the Contractor for payment under this heading. This is discussed further in Chapter 2 of this book.

No specific duties or responsibilities are allocated to the Employer.

14.6 Issue of Interim Payment Certificates

This sub-clause opens with the statement '*No amount will be certified or paid until the Employer has received and approved the Performance Security*'.

Considering that Sub-Clause 4.2, Performance Security, requires the Contractor to provide the Employer with an acceptable Performance Security within 28 days of the Contractor receiving the Letter of Acceptance (or Contract Agreement), the Employer should be in a position to give his assent expeditiously, so that the certification and subsequent payment of Interim Payment Certificates need not be delayed.

Within 28 days of receiving a Statement from the Contractor, the Engineer is required to issue an Interim Payment Certificate to the Employer with a copy to the Contractor. The period of 28 days is not to be extended because of any internal requirements of the Employer.

It may be an internal regulation of the Employer that the Contractor adds his signature to the summary sheet of an Interim Payment Certificate, even though there is no contractual requirement. Other Employers may require the Contractor to provide a commercial invoice separate to the Interim Payment Certificate for accounting purposes.

To avoid misunderstandings and delays, it would be appropriate for the Employer to advise both the Contractor and the Engineer of his requirements at an early stage of the Contract.

14.7 Payment

The Employer is obligated to pay to the Contractor:

(a) the Advance Payment (refer to Sub-Clause 14.2), provided that the Contractor has complied with the requirements of Sub-Clause 4.2 (Performance Security) and Sub-Clause 14.2 (Advance Payment)

(b) the amount certified in each Interim Payment Certificate within 56 days after the date the Engineer receives the Statement and supporting documents. It will be noted that Sub-Clause 14.6 provides that the Engineer has to issue his Interim Payment Certificate within 28 days of receipt of the Contractor's Statement. Any delay by the Engineer in providing the Interim Payment Certificate will impact on the time available for the Employer to make payment

(c) the amount certified in the Final Payment Certificate within 56 days of receipt of this Final Payment Certificate (refer to Sub-Clause 14.11).

14.8 Delayed Payment

If the Contractor does not receive payment from the Employer when due, in accordance with Sub-Clause 14.8 he is entitled '*to receive financing charges compounded monthly on the unpaid amount*'. This entitlement is irrespective of any claim the Employer may have against the Contractor. These financing charges shall be calculated based on an interest rate three percentage points above the discount rate of the central bank in the country of the currency of payment and shall be paid in such currency.

Typically the Contractor will have elected to be paid in both local and foreign currencies. Due to a lack of foreign currency, the delayed payment is most likely to occur with the foreign currency portion of the Contractor's payment entitlement.

The applicable discount rates of the major central banks are widely published.

The Contractor is not required to give notice of his entitlement to payment of these financial charges. These charges may be conveniently included as a separate item within any Interim Payment Certificate.

This sub-clause does not provide for the Contractor to claim an extension of time arising as a consequence of delayed payment.

14.9 Payment of Retention Money

Following the issue of the Taking-Over Certificate the Engineer has the duty to calculate the amount of the Retention Money to be repaid to the Contractor in the next Interim Payment Certificate (see also Appendix F).

There is no involvement of the Employer in the preparation of this calculation.

14.10 Statement at Completion

'*Within 84 days of receiving the Taking-Over Certificate for the Works, the Contractor is required to submit a Statement showing*':

- the value of work done up to the date of the Taking-Over Certificate
- any further sums which the Contractor considers to be due (including outstanding claims)
- an estimate of other amounts which may become due (including the value of any outstanding works).

There is no direct involvement of the Employer.

14.11 Application for Final Payment Certificate

'*56 days after receiving the Performance Certificate the Contractor is required to submit to the Engineer a draft Final Statement showing*':

- the value of work done
- any further sums which the Contractor considers are due to him.

The Engineer and the Contractor are required to discuss any outstanding matters in dispute (which discussions are very likely to require the involvement of the Employer) in order to reach a final agreement. If this is not possible, the Engineer shall prepare and deliver an Interim Payment Certificate to the Employer for payment and any remaining disputes shall be resolved by the DAB (Sub-Clause20.4) or by amicable settlement (Sub-Clause 20.5) or by Arbitration (Sub-Clause 20.6), which will then permit the Engineer to issue a Final Statement.

14.12 Discharge

'*When submitting the Final Statement, the Contractor shall submit a written discharge which confirms that the total of the Final Statement represents full and final settlement of all moneys due to the Contractor under or in connection with the Contract*'.

A sample form of discharge is provided in the FIDIC Contracts Guide on page 253.

14.13 Issue of Final Payment Certificate

Within 28 days after receiving the Final Statement and the written discharge, the Engineer shall issue the Final Payment Certificate and the Employer shall pay any outstanding amounts due to the Contractor with due allowance for any credits due to the Employer from the Contractor.

14.14 Cessation of Employer's Liability

The Contractor is obliged to include an item in the Final Statement (Sub-Clause 14.11) and also in the Statement on Completion (Sub-Clause 14.10) which defines any matter (including claims) that he considers to be unresolved and therefore remaining an Employer's liability.

This requirement provides a limit to the remaining liabilities of the Employer (excepting for the Employer's liability for indemnification and any liabilities arising from cases of fraud, default or misconduct).

14.15 Currencies of Payment

The Employer is required to pay the Contractor any amount due in the currencies named in the Appendix to the Tender. The exchange rates given in the Appendix to the Tender shall be applicable. If no exchange rates are given in the Appendix to the Tender, then the exchange rates prevailing on the Base Data and determined by the central bank of the country shall be applicable.

If only one currency is specified, then this sub-clause is inapplicable.

The Engineer has the primary responsibility for determining the amount of each currency due to the Contractor.

Clause 15 Termination by the Employer

15.1 Notice to Correct

'If the Contractor fails to carry out any obligation under the Contract, the Engineer may by notice require the Contractor to make good the failure and to remedy it within a specified reasonable time'.

The giving of a notice to correct by the Engineer can – in the event of continuing non-compliance by the Contractor – be regarded as a prelude to the Employer issuing a notice of Termination.

Consequently the giving of a notice to correct is an important event and should not be trivialised. As a minimum it should reference this sub-clause, identify the nature of the Contractor's failure and specify a reasonable time for the Contractor to take corrective action.

However, there is no obligation for the notice to be given under this sub-clause before the Employer terminates the Contract. The issue of a notice to correct is frequently the inevitable outcome of the Contractor persistently failing to execute the Works expeditiously and to the required standard specified in the Contract.

The Contractor should be made aware that the giving of a notice to correct by the Engineer is a significant event and that he ignores it at his own peril.

15.2 Termination by the Employer

Termination of the Contract by the Employer is evidently a serious matter and the Employer should seek legal advice prior to the giving of the notice to ensure that all legal formalities are correctly observed.

Termination of the Contract may be an inevitable consequence of non-performance by the Contractor, but it leaves the Employer with the consequential problems of having to appoint a replacement contractor with attendant delays and increases in cost. The provision of continued funding of the Contract, particularly by the international financing agencies, may be jeopardised. These negative aspects of termination have to be evaluated by the Employer prior to the issue of the termination notice.

Summarised, the Employer shall be entitled to terminate the Contract if the Contractor:

(a) (i) fails to provide a Performance Security (Sub-Clause 4.2)
    (ii) fails to comply with a Notice to Correct (Sub-Clause 15.1) or
(b) abandons the Works or
(c) (i) fails to proceed with the Works in accordance with Clause 8 (Commencement, Delays and Suspension)
    (ii) fails to comply with a notice issued under Sub-Clause 7.5 (rejection) or Sub-Clause 7.6 (Remedial Works) or
(d) subcontracts the whole of the Works or assigns the Contract without prior agreement or

(e) becomes bankrupt or insolvent or
(f) gives or offers bribes.

The Employer is required to give the Contractor 14 days' notice of termination of the Contract. However, the termination can be immediate in respect of events covered by items (e) and (f) above. The notice can be withdrawn if the Parties agree that the notice shall be of no effect.

After termination the Contractor is required to leave the Site and deliver all Goods, all Contractor's Documents and other design documents to the Engineer.

Further, this sub-clause states that *'the Employer shall then give notice that the Contractor's Equipment and Temporary Works will be released to the Contractor at or near the Site'*. In reality, the Contractor – having received notice of termination – will immediately seek to remove these items for the Site.

The on-site situation can become quite fraught and difficult as subcontractors and the Contractor's own employees will also leave the Site, carrying their own possessions. The subcontractors in particular may attempt to remove Plant and Materials which are already subject to payment made under the Contract.

Consequently, the Employer may find it necessary to immediately install his own security force both to guard the Site and to control removals. The Engineer will be in a position to advise the Employer which Plant and Materials are already the subject of payments under the Contract or which would become the subject of future payments. In any event detailed records need to be maintained for evaluation, should future disputes arise.

Even a controlled demobilisation will not necessarily clear the Site of unwanted items and scrap. Further, the Employer may elect to maintain the basic infrastructure of the Site for use by a potential replacement Contractor. This may entitle the Contractor to compensatory payments.

Finally the Employer will need to consider the need for continuation of the supply of water and electricity to the Site and make provisions for ongoing payment for these utilities.

Termination, particularly for large, more complex sites can result in complicated issues to be resolved by the Employer and it is appropriate that the Employer has in hand a detailed action plan in readiness for the termination.

In parallel with the above activities, the Employer (not the Engineer) will need to give formal notice to the providers of both the Performance Guarantee and the Advance Payment Guarantee that the Contract has been terminated and that the Employer intends to request payment in respect of additional costs consequent upon termination and/or outstanding amounts due for repayment. Initially there is no requirement for the Employer to quantify the amount requested, since this will not be immediately known.

15.3 Valuation at Date of Termination

This sub-clause requires the Engineer, as soon as practical after termination under Sub-Clause 15.2, *'to proceed in accordance with Sub-Clause 3.5, Determinations, to agree or determine the value of the Works, Goods and*

Contractor's Documents, and any other sums due to the Contractor for work executed in accordance with the Contract'.

Sub-Clause 3.5, Determinations, requires that in making his determination *'the Engineer shall consult with each Party in an endeavour to reach agreement...'*.

Consequently, the Engineer, in carrying out his duties under this sub-clause, has the duty to consult with the Parties in making his determination. Considering that there are likely to be a number of contentious items to be evaluated, including existing claims, it is quite possible that the Engineer will only be able to produce a qualified valuation at date of termination. This implies that there could be items to be finally settled by a DAB board or formal arbitration if that is practical.

Since Sub-Clause 15.3 requires the Engineer to proceed *'as soon as practical'*, it may be appropriate for the Engineer to issue his determination in sections or parts in anticipation that they may be accepted by the Parties, it being noted that there is no requirement for the Engineer to 'agree' his Determination with the Parties.

The Engineer may request confirmatory instructions from the Employer should the preparation of the valuation exceed his duties defined in his service contract.

15.4   Payment after Termination

After a notice of termination under Sub-Clause 15.2, the Employer is entitled to:

(a) *proceed to present any claims under Sub-Clause 2.5 (Employer's Claims)*
(b) *withhold further payments to the Contractor until the costs of execution completion, remedying of any defects etc. have been established*
(c) *recover from the Contractor any losses or damages incurred by the Employer and any costs of completing the Works after allowing for any amounts due to the Contractor (refer to Sub-Clause 15.3).'*

From the above it is unlikely that any further amounts will be paid to the Contractor until all costs consequent upon termination are established and finalised.

15.5   Employer's Entitlement to Termination

The Employer is entitled to terminate the Contract at any time for the Employer's convenience, by giving notice of such termination to the Contractor.

The termination takes effect 28 days after the Contractor receives the notice of termination or the Employer returns the Performance Security, whichever is the latest.

The Employer may not terminate the Contract in order to execute the Works himself or have the Works executed by another contractor.

The FIDIC Contracts Guide recommends *'In the rare event of having to invoke this Sub-Clause, the Employer should take prior legal advice'*.

Clause 16 Suspension and Termination by the Contractor

16.1 Contractor's Entitlement to Suspend Work

The Contractor's entitlement to suspend work relates to financial matters which can be summarised as follows:

(i) the failure of the Employer to provide details of his financial arrangements (Sub-Clause 2.4)
(ii) the failure of the Engineer to certify an Interim Payment Certificate (Sub-Clause 14.6)
(iii) the failure of the Employer to pay an Interim Payment Certificate when due (Sub-Clause 14.7).

The Contractor is entitled to suspend work or reduce the rate of the work 21 days after having given notice. He shall restart work as soon as possible after receiving payment.

The Contractor is entitled to an extension of time for any delay incurred and payment of any additional costs incurred as a consequence of the suspension plus profit.

16.2 Termination by the Contractor

'*The Contractor is entitled to terminate the Contract under the following circumstances*:

(a) *the Contractor does not receive reasonable evidence within 42 days after giving notice under Sub-Clause 16.1 in respect of a failure to comply with Sub-Clause 2.4 (Employer's Financial Arrangements)*
(b) *the Engineer fails, within 56 days after receiving a Statement... to issue the relevant Payment Certificate*
(c) *the Contractor does not receive the amount due under an Interim Payment Certificate within 42 days after the expiry of the time stated in Sub-Clause 14.7 (Payment)*
(d) *the Employer substantially fails to perform his obligations under the Contract*
(e) *the Employer fails to comply with Sub-Clause 1.6 (Contract Agreement) or Sub-Clause 1.7 (Assignment)*
(f) *A prolonged suspension affects the whole of the Works as described in Sub-Clause 8.11 (Prolonged Suspension)*
(g) *the Employer becomes bankrupt or insolvent, or goes into liquidation...*'

In any of these events or circumstances the Contractor may, upon giving 14 days' notice to the Employer, terminate the Contract. However, in the case of sub-paragraphs (f) or (g) the Contractor may by notice terminate the Contract immediately.

The FIDIC Contracts Guide states '*If the Contractor gives notice and then wishes to withdraw it, the Parties may agree that the notice may be of no effect and that the Contract is not terminated*'.

16.3 Cessation of Work and Removal of Contractor's Equipment

This sub-clause itemises the actions required of the Contractor in the event of his termination of the Contract:

(i) Cease all work unless instructed by the Engineer to protect life or property.
(ii) Hand over all Contractor's Documents for which the Contractor has been paid.
(iii) Remove all other Goods from Site.

16.4 Payment on Termination

'*After the notice of termination has taken effect, the Employer shall promptly*
- *return the Performance Security to the Contractor*
- *pay the Contractor in accordance with Sub-Clause 19.6*
- *pay the Contractor the amount of any loss of profit or other loss or damage sustained by the Contractor as a result of this termination.*'

The Employer is required to return the Advance Payment Guarantee to the Contractor once the Advance Payment has been repaid in full. The Employer is entitled to receive repayment of the outstanding amount of the Advance Payment immediately on termination.

Clause 17 Risk and Responsibility

17.1 Indemnities

This sub-clause requires each Party to indemnify the other Party from any claims arising out of the Contractor's execution of the Works. This obligation extends to any claims of third parties.

The Contractor

The Contractor is required to indemnify the Employer, the Employer's Personnel and their agents against and from all claims, damages, etc. in respect of:

(a) injury, sickness, disease or death of any person arising from the Contractor's execution of the Works, including any consequences arising from the Contractor's Design (if any). The Contractor is not required to provide indemnity in respect of any negligence or wilful act of the Employer, Employer's Personnel or their agents
(b) damage to or loss of property to the extent that such damage or loss
  (i) arises out of or as a consequence of the Contractor's design, the execution of the Works and the remedying of defects
  (ii) is attributable to the negligence or a wilful act of the Contractor, the Contractor's Personnel or his agents.

The Employer

The Employer is required to indemnify the Contractor, the Contractor's Personnel and their agents from all claims in respect of

(a) injury, sickness, disease or death attributable to any negligence by the Employer, the Employer's Personnel and their agents
(b) those matters for which liability may be excluded for insurance cover (refer to Sub-Clause 18.3(d)).

17.2 Contractor's Care of the Works

The Contractor is responsible for the care of the Works and Goods until the Taking-Over Certificate (for the whole or any section or any part) of the Works is issued, when responsibility passes to the Employer. After the issue of a Taking-Over Certificate the Contractor remains responsible for the care of any outstanding work until it is completed and for any damage caused by his actions in completing the outstanding work.

In the period when the Contractor is responsible for care of the Works, should a loss or damage occur, then the Contractor is obliged to rectify the loss or damage at his own cost, unless it can be demonstrated that the loss or damage arose as a consequence of a risk attributable to the Employer.

The FIDIC Contracts Guide comments that it is important to precisely define the geographical extent of anything taken over by the Employer, in order that the Party having responsibility is clearly identifiable. The use of marked-up drawings may be a useful and convenient means of recording the extent of a taking over by the Employer.

17.3   Employer's Risks

Employer's risks (which may also be Force Majeure events) are identified in this sub-clause as:

(a)   *war, hostilities, invasion, act of foreign enemies*
(b)   *rebellion, terrorism, revolution, civil war within the Country*
(c)   *riot, commotion, disorder in the Country by persons other than the Contractor's Personnel and other employees*
(d)   *munitions of war, explosive materials…*
(e)   *pressure waves caused by aircraft…*
(f)   *use of occupation by the Employer of any part of the Permanent Works, unless specified in the Contract*
(g)   *design of any part of the Works by the Employer's Personnel or other for whom the Employer is responsible*
(h)   *forces of nature which were Unforeseeable or against which an experienced contractor could not reasonably have been expected to have taken adequate preventative precautions*'.

Note: With reference to (h) above, adverse climatic conditions are specifically excluded from the scope of Sub-Clause 4.12 'Unforeseeable Physical Conditions' and consequently such matters need to be referred to this Sub-Clause.

17.4   Consequences of Employer's Risks

In the event of the occurrence of an Employer's Risk as listed in Sub-Clause 17.3, the Contractor is required to give notice to the Engineer in accordance with the procedures stated in Sub-Clause 20.1. The Contractor is entitled to an extension of Time for Completion and payment of his Costs plus profit. If the occurrence results in loss or damage to the Works, then the Contractor is entitled to receive instructions from the Engineer.

17.5   Intellectual and Industrial Property Rights

The Employer is required to indemnify the Contractor from any claim alleging an infringement which results from the Contractor's compliance with the Contract or which arises from the Employer using the Works for purposes not indicated in the Contract or its use in conjunction with anything not supplied by the Contractor.

The Contractor is required to indemnify the Employer against any claim which arises out of the manufacture, use, sale or import of any Goods or design for which the Contractor is responsible.

The Employer is obligated to give notice to the Contractor within 28 days of having received a claim from a third party alleging infringement.

17.6 Limitation of Liability

Neither Party is liable to the other Party for any consequential losses.

The total liability of the Contractor to the Employer in connection with the Contract (exceptions are noted) shall not exceed the sum indicated in the Particular Conditions or (if a sum is not so stated) the Accepted Contract Amount.

The Employer's liability is subject to the provisions of Sub-Clause 14.14, Cessation of Employer's Liability.

The FIDIC Contracts Guide notes that the application of this sub-clause may be limited by the applicable law.

Clause 18 Insurance

18.1 General Requirements for Insurances

In the preparation of the Tender Documents the Employer is required to specify his insurance requirements in detail. The Employer will need to specify who will be the 'insuring Party' for each category of insurance required by the terms of the Contract.

Whenever the Contractor is designated as the insuring Party, each insurance shall be effected with insurers and in terms approved by the Employer. These terms shall be consistent with the requirements given in the Contract Documents (or as may be otherwise agreed between the Employer and the Contractor prior to the issue of the Letter of Acceptance or signing of the Contract).

For complex projects, where the Employer intends to enter into a number of separate contracts, the Employer may find it convenient and more economical to arrange for himself the required insurances. These Employer-provided insurances will be designed to provide insurance cover to all the contracts forming the project in its totality. In making his arrangements for the Contract insurances, the Employer should ensure that the insurances make provision for payment in foreign currencies where appropriate. The insurance premiums will in part be determined by the amount of policy excesses. The Employer will need to advise tenderers of the value of these policy excesses, so that they may make allowance for any non-reimbursable excess in their tender price.

Whenever the Parties are to be jointly insured, then each Party has the right to submit his own claims under the terms of the insurance policy. In such cases the insurer will most likely be required to make payments directly to the Party making the claim. Alternatively the Contract Documents may require that all insurance payments shall be paid into a special bank account created for the sole purpose of receiving insurance payments, which is to be jointly administered by the Parties. Any distribution from the special bank account is subject to the approval of both Parties.

Each Party shall be entitled to receive evidence from the insuring Party, confirming that insurance premiums are properly maintained throughout the period of the Contract.

It is recommended that the insuring Party uses the services of a specialist advisor, well experienced in this type of insurance, to negotiate the detail of the terms and conditions of the insurances with the proposed insurer.

18.2 Insurance for Works and Contractor's Equipment

The wording of this Sub-Clause 18.12 assumes that the Contractor will be the insuring Party and will require modification should the Employer decide that he will be the insuring Party.

This requirement covers two differing categories of insurance which can be taken separately.

(a) Insurance for Works

The insuring Party shall insure the Works, Plant, Materials and Contractor's Documents for not less than the full reinstatement costs. This type of insurance is frequently referred to as 'Contractor's All Risk' (or CAR) insurance. The insurance premium is likely to be calculated as a percentage of the Accepted Contract Amount and consequently the Employer may consider it appropriate to specify that the Contractor shall ensure that the amount of the insurance shall be for the Accepted Contract Amount plus an additional percentage (often 15%) to cover the likely cost of additional works which may be required and any subsequent inflationary increases in cost. The wording of the insurance policy shall cover the full cost of reinstatement of the cost of damage or loss to the Works, including the cost of any demolition, debris removal, and engineering costs. Policy excesses are to be stated.

The insuring Party shall maintain this insurance until the date of issue of the Performance Certificate, to cover any loss or damage arising from a cause for which the Contractor is liable prior to the date of issue of the Taking-Over Certificate and any loss or damage caused by the Contractor during any other operations, included those operations undertaken during the Defects Liability Period.

(b) Contractor's Equipment

The insuring Party shall insure the Contractor's Equipment for not less than the full replacement cost, including delivery to site.

Where the Contractor is nominated as the insuring Party, he may elect to provide this type of insurance in one of a number of ways:

(i) by obtaining the insurance from a suitable provider covering only the specific needs of the Contract

(ii) many international contractors operate a plant pool from which the individual contracts lease equipment. To facilitate the movement of equipment, it is likely that the Contractor already has continuous insurance covering all his equipment. Thus the Contractor may have no need to obtain a separate insurance specific to any given project. The Contractor will be required to provide appropriate evidence of his arrangements

(iii) larger projects are more likely to be executed by joint ventures formed solely for the purpose of executing the Contract. The sponsor company of the joint venture will arrange the required insurance on behalf of the joint venture.

Sub-Clause 18.2 further states, inter alia, that these insurances shall cover all loss and damage from any cause not listed in Sub-Clause 17.3, Employer's Risks, but excludes any part of the Works taken over by the Employer (excepting defects liability operations) and any loss or damage to a part of the Works which is defective as a consequence of a design defect (where the Contractor is not responsible for the design).

It is preferable that the Contractor includes for insurance of the Subcontractor's Equipment within the scope of his insurance. This is a convenient arrangement, since the Contractor may not have established the full scope of Subcontractor involvement.

Some subcontractors may prefer to provide their own insurances, but these will need constant monitoring by the Contractor to ensure compliance with the requirements of the Contract and consequently is not an administratively convenient arrangement.

In contrast, very large specialised items of Subcontractor Equipment, e.g. very large cranes, may be on site for a very limited period and it would be convenient for the Subcontractor to provide the required insurances.

18.3 Insurance against Injury to Persons and Damage to Property

The Insuring Party is required to *'insure against each Party's liability for any loss, damage, death or bodily injury which may occur to any physical property (except things insured under Sub-Clause 18.4) which may arise out of the Contractor's performance of the Contract...'*
and
'This insurance shall be for a limit per occurrence of the amount stated in the Appendix to Tender, with no limit on the number of occurrences.'

Additionally the insurance shall *'cover liability for loss or damage to the Employer's property (excluding things insured under Sub-Clause 18.2) arising out of the Contractor's performance of the Contract'*, but excludes:

- the Employer's right to execute the Permanent Works on, over and under any land, and to occupy this land
- damage unavoidably caused by the Contractor executing the Works
- a cause listed in Sub-Clause 17.3, Employer's Risks.

18.4 Insurance for Contractor's Personnel

The Contractor is responsible to provide insurance against any liability for claims, losses, etc. arising from claims, losses, etc. which may arise from injury, sickness, disease or death of any of his employees for the full period the personnel are on site. Subcontractors may provide their own separate insurances, but the Contractor is responsible to ensure they comply with the requirements of this sub-clause.

In many countries the provision of this type of insurance is likely to be a legal obligation. As a general rule, international contractors provide appropriate insurance for their expatriate personnel as part of their employment package, independently of the country in which they are employed. Local workers are likely to be insured as required by local law, which obligation may be supplemented by the Contractor as an employment inducement.

Clause 19 Force Majeure

19.1 Definition of Force Majeure

This sub-clause of the Contract notes that '*in the laws of most countries, a Party may be relieved from its contractual obligations in a very narrow range of events*'. However, in the FIDIC contract forms '*the expression "Force Majeure" has a more broadly defined meaning, namely an exceptional event or circumstance..*' which satisfies the following criteria:

- *must be beyond the control of the Party who has been affected by it and who will need to give due notice (Sub-Clause 19.2)*
- *the affected Party could not reasonably have provided against it before the Contract was made*
- *the affected Party could not reasonably have avoided or overcome it*
- *it must not have been substantially attributable to the other Party (which may for example include breach of Contract by such other Party, entitling the affected party to more favourable relief due to the breach of Contract.*

The FIDIC Contracts Guide emphasises that for an event or circumstance to constitute Force Majeure it must be 'exceptional' and not merely 'unusual'. Whether it is unforeseeable is irrelevant.

The text of this sub-clause provides an illustrative list of events or circumstances which would constitute Force Majeure. Other events or circumstances may constitute Force Majeure provided that they fulfil the criteria listed above.

19.2 Notice of Force Majeure

If a Party is or will be prevented from performing any obligations under the Contract, then the Party shall give notice to the other Party within 14 days of the event or circumstance constituting the Force Majeure. Note that this 14 days' notice period differs from the 28 days' notice period for claims notified in accordance with Sub-Clause 20.1.

The Party giving the notice shall identify which obligations are prevented.

19.3 Duty to Minimise Delay

Each Party has a duty to minimise delays arising as a result of Force Majeure. A Party shall give notice to the other Party once the cause of Force Majeure ceases.

19.4 Consequences of Force Majeure

Having given notice of Force Majeure, the Contractor is entitled to claim an extension of Time for Completion (Sub-Clause 8.4) and to payment of Costs (Sub-Clause 19.1 (i) to (iv)).

19.5 Force Majeure Affecting Subcontractor

Should the terms of a Subcontract entitle a Subcontractor to relief on additional and/or broader terms than are available to the Contractor under the Contract, then the Contractor is not entitled to rely on the Subcontract to provide relief under the Contract.

19.6 Optional Termination, Payment and Release

'*If the execution of substantially all of the Works is prevented for a continuous period of 84 days by reason of Force Majeure or multiple periods totalling more than 140 days due to the same Force Majeure, then either Party may give the other Party notice of termination of the Contract*'. Termination shall take place 7 days after the giving of the notice.

Thereafter the Engineer shall value the work done and issue a Payment Certificate to include:

- all work done at Contract Prices
- the cost of Plant and Materials delivered or ordered
- all other cost or liability… reasonably incurred in anticipation of executing the Works
- the cost of repatriating the Contractor's labour and staff.

19.7 Release from Performance by Law

If any event or circumstance including Force Majeure makes it impossible or unlawful for either Party to fulfil their contractual obligations or which under the governing law entitles the Parties to be released from further performance, then upon notice being given by one Party to the other Party

- the Parties shall be released from further performance
- the sum payable to the Contractor shall be evaluated as described in Sub-Clause 19.6.

Clause 20 Claims, Disputes and Arbitration

20.1 Contractor's Claims

This sub-clause describes the procedure to be followed by the Contractor in the presentation of his claims. There is no direct involvement by the Employer in the administration of these procedures. The FIDIC Contracts Guide comments, inter alia, that in the event of the Contractor giving notice of claim, this should not be regarded as *'an aggressive act… but merely as an act which enables the Employer to be aware of the possibility of the Contractor's enhanced entitlement'*.

20.2 Appointment of the Dispute Adjudication Board (DAB)

In the preparation of the tender documents, the Employer has to give consideration to the composition of the DAB entrusted to promote a resolution of disputes.

The FIDIC Conditions of Contract describe three different procedures:

- *'a "full term" DAB which comprises one or three members and which is to be appointed before the Contractor commences executing of the Works*
- *an ad hoc DAB, which comprises one or three members who are only appointed if and when a particular dispute arises'*
- the engagement of an independent consulting engineer with appropriate experience and able to prepare a pre-arbitral award.

In deciding which of these alternatives shall be specified in the tender documents, the Employer and his advisors will need to take into account a number of factors:

- If the initial stages of a contract are concerned largely with off site manufacturing and not site work, the choice of composition of the DAB could be delayed or restricted to one member.
- Projects requiring major or difficult excavations, including tunnelling work, are more likely to give rise to disputes falling under the scope of Sub-Clause 4.12, Unforeseeable Physical Conditions. The early appointment of a three member DAB is appropriate.
- The commencement of site operations including site hand-over and the provision of access to site frequently give rise to delays, particularly in built-up areas and areas with security restrictions. These difficulties are amplified by delays in expropriation procedures, even if the delayed expropriation is limited to a relatively small portion of the Site. The early appointment of a three member DAB is appropriate.
- If it is anticipated that there will be a large number of variations and re-measurement issues, the more likely a three member DAB is appropriate.
- The greater the magnitude of the Contract, the greater the likelihood a three member DAB is required. As a rough guide, The FIDIC Contracts

Guide proposes if the value of the monthly Payment Certificate exceeds a range of two to three million US dollars (at year 2000 prices), then a three member DAB is more likely to be appropriate.
- Should the Parties be of different nationalities, FIDIC considers that a DAB is more effective if the DAB members are of different nationalities to the Parties and to each other.

The choice of DAB members may in any event be restricted by the experience and training of the prospective members in arbitration procedures and by language abilities.

Evidently it is preferable that the DAB is selected and functional as soon as practical after the Contract is awarded. However, the selection of board members and conclusion of their service agreements do require time to execute. The time for execution could be reduced if both the Employer and the Contractor were to nominate their preferred members in the tender documents. For single member DABs some Employers often do nominate the selected member. This may be convenient and economical, but does depart from the concept of the appointment being subject to consensus between the Parties and can raise Contractor suspicions of collusion between the Employer and the member.

A principal feature of the three member DAB is that the Parties, having nominated their proposed member (and had the same accepted by the other Party), leave the two selected members to agree and nominate a third member, who is most likely to act as the Chairman of the Board, for the approval of the Parties.

20.3 Failure to Agree Dispute Adjudication Board

In the event that the sole member of a one member DAB or one member of a three member DAB has to be replaced, the Parties shall agree a replacement member.

Should the Parties be unable to agree the appointment of a replacement member, then the appointing entity named in the Appendix to Tender (e.g. FIDIC, Institute of Civil Engineers [ICE], London) shall, after consultation, be requested to nominate the replacement member.

Both FIDIC and ICE have available a list of dispute adjudicators for consideration.

20.4 Obtaining Dispute Adjudication Board's (DAB) Decision

1   No matter can be referred for a formal decision of the DAB unless the matter is in dispute. Consequently, if a Party refers a matter to the DAB and this is disputed by the other Party, then the DAB must first consider if a dispute exists. Typically a claim will have been notified under Sub-Clause 2.5, Employer's Claims, or Sub-Clause 20.1, Contractor's Claims, and will have been subject to determination by the Engineer in

accordance with Sub-Clause 3.5, Determinations. If then there is no agreement reached, a dispute exists and either Party is entitled to request the DAB to make a decision on the matter.

Such referral to the DAB has to be in writing, in accordance with the directions of the DAB who will hear the respective pleadings of the Parties at a formal hearing.

After completion of the formal hearing, the DAB will privately consider their findings and in due course will provide the Parties with their decision.

2. As part of their routine visits to site, the DAB is likely to ask the Parties if there are any matters affecting or likely to affect the execution of the Contract, to which either Party would like to draw their attention. The DAB may be willing to offer informal advice or opinion on any matter (including claims), with the intention of encouraging the Parties to find ways and means of settling disputes without recourse to requesting a formal decision from the DAB.

3. Strict time limits apply to an application for a formal decision of the DAB.
   (a) Firstly the DAB will establish a date by which all documentation forming the presentations of the Parties has to be provided. The DAB will consider if a formal hearing is required and, where necessary and after consultation, will notify the Parties of the date of the hearing.
   (b) The DAB is required to give its directions within 84 days of receiving a referral from a Party. This period may be varied if the Parties are in agreement.
   (c) After the DAB has given its decision, each Party has a further 28 days to give notice of its dissatisfaction.

The Employer must ensure that the submissions to the DAB are not only correctly prepared to a high standard, but are presented by a date set by the DAB.

The Engineer will be a key part of the Employer's team and will be able to provide detailed information on behalf of the Employer.

The quality of presentation of the Employer's case to the DAB is important and may require that suitable additional staff is available to oversee the preparation and presentation of the Employer's case.

20.5 Amicable Settlement

Where a Party has given notice of dissatisfaction under the provisions of Sub-Clause 20.4, both Parties are required to attempt to settle the dispute amicably before commencing arbitration. There is no formal role for the Engineer in this procedure, although the Employer is likely to use his services as an advisor.

There may be a number of discussions and meetings following a Party giving notice of dissatisfaction and it may not always be clear if the process of amicable discussion has taken place or indeed has been completed. Consequently a degree of formality, recording that amicable discussion has taken place is appropriate, particularly if there is no settlement.

20.6   Arbitration

Unless settled amicably, any dispute in respect of which the DABs decision has not become final shall be finally settled by international arbitration.

The cost of arbitration will be significantly greater than the similar process already conducted by a DAB. Consequently both Parties will have to balance the likelihood of obtaining a more satisfactory conclusion in arbitration against the likely cost of arbitration. Essentially it is necessary for the Party requesting arbitration to judge whether the arbitration panel will provide an award that is more or less satisfactory than that provided by the comparable members of the DAB. It has been claimed that DAB have been successful in resolving approximately 90% of the disputes referred to them for their decision.

20.7   Failure to comply with Dispute Adjudication Board's Decision

If neither Party has given notice of dissatisfaction within the prescribed period, the decision becomes final and binding. In the event that a Party fails to give effect to the decision, then the other Party may refer this failure to arbitration without referring further to the DAB.

20.8   Expiry of Dispute Adjudication Board's Appointment

If a dispute arises and there is no DAB in place for whatever reason, either Party may refer the dispute directly to arbitration in accordance with Sub-Clause 20.6, Arbitration, without reconvening the DAB.

Chapter 2

The Engineer and the FIDIC Conditions of Contract for Construction (CONS) – 'The Red Book'

Chapter 2

The Engineer and the FIDIC Conditions of Contract for Construction (CONS) – 'The Red Book'

Introduction

Conventionally, the Engineer has two principal duties to fulfil. Firstly, there is the Engineer who designs the Works and prepares the Contract Documents on behalf of the Employer in accordance with his directions. This role of the Engineer is not a subject of the standard FIDIC forms. Nonetheless, the quality and accuracy of the Contract Documents will have a profound effect on the execution phase of the Works. The design role of the Engineer is not discussed further in this book.

The second primary role of the Engineer is the supervision of the construction phase of the project on behalf of the Employer. It is a role that is most likely to be undertaken by a different engineering company to that which was engaged to design the Works. This supervisory role of the Engineer is described and defined in detail in the standard FIDIC forms and is discussed further in this chapter.

The Engineer is not a party to the Contract. His services are engaged by and paid for by the Employer and it is inevitable that the Engineer will be subject to the overall authority of the Employer.

Consequently, to provide balance to the Contract, the standard FIDIC forms do provide the Engineer with duties and responsibilities to fulfil in respect of arbitral matters, although these are reduced from those included in previous standard FIDIC forms.

The funding for many projects is frequently provided by one or more of the international financing agencies, such as World Bank, EBRD, etc., who require strict budgetary control over the funds loaned or granted. As a consequence it is now a common feature that the Employer will have modified the General Conditions of Contract by including in the Particular Conditions restrictions in respect of the powers of the Engineer to authorise variations (Clause 13) and the award of extensions of time.

These limitations can themselves cause bureaucratic delays to the administration of projects and this aspect will be discussed in the text of this chapter.

An Employer's and Engineer's Guide to the FIDIC Conditions of Contract, First Edition. Michael D. Robinson.
© 2013 John Wiley & Sons, Ltd. Published 2013 by John Wiley & Sons, Ltd.

Clause 1 General Provisions

1.1 Definitions

The reader is referred to commentary made under this heading in Chapter 1 Sub-Clause 1.1 of this book. The descriptions of other words and phrases included in the 'Glossary of Contract Terminology' provided in the FIDIC Contracts Guide are also useful, as they give definitions of many words and phrases in common use in the construction industry.

Sub-Clause 1.1.2.4   Engineer
This sub-clause provides a definition of the Engineer:

'"Engineer" means the person appointed by the Employer to act as the Engineer for the purposes of the Contract and named in the Appendix to Tender..... .'

1.3 Communications

Although the means of communication will be stated in the Contract Documents, the Engineer will need to liaise with both Parties and ensure that his own communication systems are compatible with those of the Parties.

1.4 Law and Language

It is likely that the Employer will (with some exceptions) require that the Engineer communicates with him in the official language of the country, whereas communications with the Contractor will be in the language stated in the Appendix to Tender. Translation services will be required.

1.8 Care and Supply of Documents

It is the duty of the Employer (not the Engineer) to supply to the Contractor copies of the Contract and subsequent drawings. The Engineer will also require copies of the same documents and will also require to know precisely what documents have been provided to the Contractor by the Employer.

The Contractor is required to supply the Engineer with six copies of each of the Contractor's Documents. Although not specifically stated, there is an assumption that the Engineer will make any distribution required by the Employer.

1.9 Delayed Drawings or Instructions

The design office responsible for the production of drawings will have prepared a listing of drawings required for the execution of the Works. The Contractor will need a 'lead time' from the date of receipt of drawings in order for him to make his preparations (including the supply of materials and temporary works) prior to the physical commencement of the work covered by the drawings.

If a standard lead time for the supply of drawings can be agreed between the Engineer and the Contractor this will assist the design office to correctly prioritise their work and will minimise the possibility of missing or late drawings delaying the Contractor's activities. Should the Engineer also be the designer, such an agreement will have enhanced value.

In the event that the Contractor is delayed or likely to be delayed by the late issue of drawings or instructions, then he shall give written notice to the Engineer in accordance with the procedures described in Sub-Clause 20.1.

The Contractor is entitled to claim an extension of Time for Completion in respect of any delay and payment of additional cost plus profit.

1.13 Compliance with Statutes, Regulations and Laws

Although the Engineer is not directly involved in this subject, he will inevitably become involved as and when there are delays in obtaining the various permissions. Given the likelihood that any delays will lead to claims from the Contractor, it is important that the Engineer obtains appropriate information and instruction from the Employer.

Clause 2 The Employer

2.1 Right of Access to the Site

This sub-clause requires the Employer to provide the Contractor with not only access to the Site, but also the Site itself. Although this sub-clause does not provide for any direct involvement of the Engineer, it is most likely that the Employer will require the assistance of the Engineer to ensure a disciplined, satisfactory hand-over. Detailed records of any hand-over should be prepared and signed by the Parties.

The need for a disciplined hand-over is particularly important if the hand-over is partial and thus incomplete. The Contractor, even if he is agreeable to start work, may be reluctant to accept a partial hand-over without a firm date for finalisation of the hand-over. He may also consider himself entitled to additional payment and/or an extension of time as a consequence of the partial hand-over.

Delayed or unplanned partial hand-overs occur with surprising frequency and are particularly disruptive during the initial stages of the Contract. Detailed records of any disruption need to be maintained, preferably with the co-operation of the Contractor.

In the event of a delayed hand-over, the Contractor is required to follow the procedures described in Sub-Clause 20.1 and is entitled to claim an extension of Time for Completion in respect of any delay and payment of additional costs plus profit.

2.5 Employer's Claims

Should the Employer consider himself entitled to any payment from the Contractor under any clause of the Contract, either the Employer (or the Engineer on behalf of the Employer) shall give notice and particulars to the Contractor. A full listing of the Clauses which entitle the Employer to claim is given in Appendix D.

There is no time limit set for the presentation of Employer's claims. This sub-clause states *'The Notice shall be given as soon as practicable after the Employer became aware of the event or circumstance giving rise to the claim…'*. The time limits for Contractor's claims are stated in Sub-Clause 20.1 and further discussion on this topic is provided in Chapter 1, Sub-Clause 2.5.

Clause 3 The Engineer

3.1 Engineer's Duties and Authority

The Employer is required to formally appoint the Engineer either by the inclusion of the details of the Engineer in the Contract Documents or by formal letter to the Contractor at a later date. The Engineer shall be deemed to act for the Employer. The Engineer has no authority to amend the Contract but may *'exercise the authority attributable to the Engineer as specified in or necessarily to be implied from the Contract'*.

The Engineer shall not relieve the Contractor from any responsibilities he has under the Contract, including responsibility for errors, omissions and similar.

The sub-clause continues *'If the Engineer is required to obtain the approval of the Employer before exercising a specified authority, the requirements shall be as stated in the Particular Conditions'*.

The Particular Conditions frequently require that the Engineer obtains the agreement of the Employer before

(a) awarding an extension of time (Sub-Clause 8.4)
(b) authorising any additional payment to the Contractor (whether in settlement of claims or by variations).

However, should the Engineer exercise an authority requiring the approval of the Employer, then the Employer shall be deemed to have given approval.

3.2 Delegation by the Engineer

The Engineer is permitted to *'assign duties and delegate authority to assistants'* at the various levels of his organisation.

The Engineer will routinely delegate some part of his authority to a principal assistant, conventionally referred to as the 'Resident Engineer'. The Engineer is obliged to inform the Contractor the extent of the authority delegated to the Resident Engineer (Model letter ENG.3.2 Appendix J).

An organisation chart of the Engineer's staff is a convenient means of describing which titles, duties and responsibilities are allocated to each member of the Engineer's staff. For the more senior assistants it is appropriate that their duties and responsibilities (and any limitations thereto) are fully described not only for the understanding of the Engineer's assistants themselves, but also for the understanding of the Contractor and Employer who should be formally advised.

It would be beneficial if the Engineer's organisation were to be of a similar pattern to that of the Contractor, but this may not always be practical. It is important that the limitations of any delegation are clearly stated in order to avoid misunderstandings. Frequently the Engineer will retain all duties and responsibilities relating to key issues, typically including taking over, extensions of time and claim settlements, since these issues are of primary importance which may also require the consent of the Employer.

Unless specifically agreed by the Parties, the Engineer may not delegate his authority to determine any matter in accordance with Sub-Clause 3.5, Determinations.

The FIDIC Contracts Guide emphasises that *'whenever an assistant acts in accordance with a delegated power, the act has the same effect as though it had been performed by the Engineer'*.

3.3 Instructions of the Engineer

The contents of this sub-clause complement the preceding Sub-Clause 3.2.

'The Engineer may issue to the Contractor (at any time) instructions and additional or modified Drawings which may be necessary for the execution of the Works and the remedying of defects.'

and

'The Contractor shall only take instructions from the Engineer, or from an assistant to whom the appropriate authority has been delegated…'

The Contractor is obligated to comply with the instructions of the Engineer or delegated assistant whose instructions should be preferably given in writing (if practical, the use of field instruction books is recommended for minor instructions between field staff, as their use will minimise oral instructions the intent of which may be the subject of dispute at a later date).

Should the Engineer or delegated assistant give an oral instruction, which is confirmed in writing by the Contractor within two working days of receiving the instruction and is not countermanded within a further two working days, then the confirmation shall constitute the written instruction of the Engineer or delegated assistant.

3.5 Determinations

Clauses permitting the Contractor to claim additional payment or additional Time for Completion are distributed throughout the Conditions of Contract. Descriptions of the various clauses which the Contractor is permitted to claim under are given under the appropriate clause headings and are listed in Appendix E.

Sub-Clause 20.1 describes in detail the procedure to be followed by the Contractor, should he consider himself entitled to additional payment, an extension of time or both. It is crucial that the Contractor adheres to the time limitations given in that sub-clause.

Provided that the Contractor has correctly followed the procedural requirements of Sub-Clause 20.1, the Engineer is required to formally respond within the stated time limit of 42 days (also stated in Sub-Clause 20.1) with approval or disapproval and detailed comments.

The Engineer may require the Contractor to provide additional information ('detailed particulars'), but is required to respond on the principles of the claim within the stated period of 42 days.

Sub-Clause 3.5 requires the Engineer to agree or determine any matter under the Contract and is the formal response to any claim raised by the Contractor.

It is noted that Sub-Clause 3.2 prohibits the Engineer from delegating his authority under this Sub-Clause.

The FIDIC Contracts Guide summarises the procedures to be followed by the Engineer in preparing his Determination. The Engineer is firstly required to consult with both Parties, separately or individually, and make every effort to achieve the agreement of both Parties and not with one Party only. If the agreement of both Parties cannot be achieved within a reasonable period of time, the Engineer is then required to make a 'fair Determination in accordance with the Contract', which he has then to notify to the Parties. This Determination is binding upon both Parties, unless revised under the Dispute Adjudication Board (DAB) procedure (refer to Clause 20). It is quite possible that the Engineer will issue an interim Determination with the intention to finalise the matter if and when more detailed particulars become available.

In respect of Sub-Clause 3.1 'Engineer's Duties and Authority' it is noted that the authority of the Engineer is frequently amended in the Particular Conditions of Contract. Frequently the Engineer is not permitted to authorise additional payment without the prior agreement of the Employer. Consequently, there is potential conflict between the Engineer's obligations contained in Sub-Clauses 3.5 and 20.1 and those given in the Particular Conditions of Contract. It may be assumed that the Engineer will not make a Determination awarding additional payment or an extension of time to the Contractor without having obtained the prior agreement of the Employer.

The FIDIC Contracts Guide recommends that if the Engineer is an independent consulting engineer who is to act impartially, the following should be added at the end of the first paragraph of Sub-Clause 3.5: '.... *The Engineer shall act impartially when making these determinations*'. Such wording will negate any restrictions placed on the Engineer in authorising additional payments to the Contractor.

Correct and timely payment of amounts due to him is the lifeblood of the Contractor. The Employer, having restricted the powers and authority of the Engineer, has an obligation to ensure any potential payment delays are minimised and conflict avoided.

Clause 4 The Contractor

4.1 Contractor's General Obligations

The Contractor is required to provide everything necessary for his design, execution, completion and remedying of defects.

- The Contractor shall provide the Plant and all Contractor's Personnel, Goods, consumables and services, whether of a temporary or permanent nature, necessary for the design, execution, completion and remedying of defects.
- The Contract must specify the scope of the Contractor's design (if any). Design requirements will be broadly described and the overriding consideration given in the FIDIC Contracts Guide is that the design '... *is for the purposes for which it is intended as specified in the Contract*'. The Contractor shall submit '*as built documents, operation and maintenance manuals in sufficient detail for the Employer to operate, maintain and repair this part of the Works*'.

It will be noted that the Contractor's obligations to produce 'as built documents' (which would include the so-called as built drawings) is limited to documents arising from the scope of the Contractor's design. There is no obligation in this sub-clause for the Contractor to produce as built documents for the full scope of the Works (as would be if the Works were to be constructed under a FIDIC P & DB form of Contract – the 'Yellow Book').

4.2 Performance Security

The Engineer will be available to provide the Employer with any assistance he may need in the management of the Performance Security. He will be best placed to check that the Contractor is continuing to maintain the Performance Security in accordance with the Contract.

Typical difficulties which may arise in the administration of the Performance Security are highlighted in Chapter 1, Sub-Clause 4.2 of this book.

4.3 Contractor's Representative

Frequently the Contractor has to provide the name and particulars of the Contractor's Representative with his tender. Difficulties can arise because the proposed person subsequently leaves the employment of the Contractor or, as not infrequently is the case, is no longer available because the award and subsequent commencement of the Works is significantly delayed. In the case of such an event the Contractor is required to submit the '*name and particulars of another suitable person…*' for the position.

If the Contractor's Representative is not named in the tender, then directly after a Letter of Acceptance is issued, the Contractor is required to submit the name and particulars of the proposed Contractor's Representative to the Engineer for consent (not approval). The Employer is likely to review the particulars of the proposed candidate.

The appointment of the Contractor's Representative is an important event of contractual significance. The Contractor should ensure that in addition to his formal appointment he is correctly introduced to both the Employer and the Engineer. Similarly, if the Contractor's Representative is to be replaced or withdraws, the Employer and the Engineer should be informed well in advance in order that the appointment of the replacement can follow smoothly without disappointment to either Party.

It has to be recognised that regardless of the definitive statements contained in the Contract, neither the Employer nor the Engineer nor the Contractor will allow delegation of powers to their representatives that will materially endanger or destabilise their commercial or legal interests.

The Contractor's Representative can delegate any powers or authority to any '*competent person*'. This has parallels to delegation of powers or authority by the Engineer to a delegated assistant (cross-refer to Sub-Clause 3.2). The Contractor's Representative should approach this subject most carefully, with particular reference to Sub-Clause 1.3 'Communications'.

A detailed organogram of both the Engineer's and Contractor's staffing arrangements is an important tool in ensuring that everyone is aware of 'who is doing what'.

4.4 Subcontractors

The Contractor is not entitled to subcontract the whole of the Works. A limit to the amount which can be subcontracted may be given in the Contract Documents. It is possible that the Employer or Engineer may from time to time require evidence of compliance by the Contractor.

'*The Contractor is responsible for the acts and defaults of the Subcontractors (including his agents and employees) as if they were acts and defaults of the Contractor.*'

The Contractor is required to obtain the prior consent of the Engineer to subcontract parts of the Works with the proviso that no approval is required in respect of suppliers of materials and subcontractors who are named in the Contract.

Frequently and particularly at the commencement of the Contract an application for consent and the giving of consent (or otherwise) has to be dealt with expeditiously if delays are to be avoided. An early discussion between Engineer and Contractor to establish the handling of applications, the extent of documentation and similar would be beneficial.

The Engineer may have difficulty in restraining the Contractor to adhere to the stated subcontracting limits stated in the Contract. Consequently it would be useful if the Engineer were to demand that the anticipated value of any subcontract be included in any application for consent. It may be difficult for the Engineer to decide if an organisation is a subcontractor requiring consent or a supplier not requiring consent.

There are administrative advantages to be gained by the Contractor if he can identify at least key subcontractors and suppliers in his tender offer. However, these advantages have to be balanced against the reliability of the subcontractor and his willingness to give financial commitments far in advance of the actual performance of the subcontract works.

A tender requirement for contractors to specify their subcontractors can give rise to difficulties in some Middle Eastern countries, where the business culture is different from that in the West. Having been awarded a contract in which it is obligatory to name his subcontractors, the Contractor is placed in considerable difficulty if those subcontractors decline or are unable to enter into a formal subcontract or take advantage of the situation by significantly increasing their tender offers, The Contractor often will find it difficult and time consuming to obtain the agreement of the Employer to change the subcontractor, since this most likely will lead to technical changes. The natural suspicion is that the Contractor wishes to change subcontractors for his own financial benefit. A considerable effort may be required to allay the concerns of the Employer. This can be complex, since the Contractor may be required to provide a technical comparison between subcontractor products. Should the two subcontractor suppliers use different national technical standards, then the comparison is made even more onerous.

Clearly, if the Contractor is obliged or wishes to identify his proposed subcontractors in his tender offer, he should make every effort to deal with reputable reliable subcontractors, especially those with whom he has dealt with previously.

4.5 Assignment of Benefit of Subcontract

The extent of any assignment permitted or required is to be described in the Contract Documents.

At the date of taking over of the Works (or section or part thereof) it may be a contractual requirement that a subcontractor continues to provide further services for an extended period. The Engineer will be required to ensure that the arrangements for assignment are formalised between the Employer, the Contractor and the subcontractor.

4.6 Co-operation

This sub-clause requires the Contractor to allow opportunities for the Employer's personnel, other contractors employed by the Employer and the personnel of public authorities to carry out work on the site.

In principle these requirements should be identified in the tender documents and the Contractor should make his prices accordingly. These requirements may have a programming impact and this should also be recorded so that in the event of individual delays, the consequential delay to the Completion Date can be ascertained and responsibility allocated.

Should the degree of the co-operation be extended or enlarged in excess of that identified in the tender documents, the Engineer is required to issue instructions to the Contractor. '*The Engineer's instruction shall constitute a Variation if and to the extent it causes the Contractor to incur Unforeseeable Cost.*' FIDIC is silent in respect of the possibility that the Engineer's instruction may cause delays which would entitle the Contractor to an extension of time. Nonetheless, the Contractor should give notice of a claim if such an event occurs.

It is further stated that the services to be provided by the Contractor under this sub-clause may include '*the use of Contractor's Equipment, Temporary Works or access arrangements, which are the responsibility of the Contractor*'.

The use of the Contractor's Equipment by others would entitle the Contractor to corresponding payment. This provision may also disrupt the Contractor's own activities, entitling the Contractor to an extension of time. The Engineer should be requested to adjudicate if there is a conflict.

Temporary Works or access arrangements refer to use of scaffolding, access ladders, walkways and access roads already provided by the Contractor for his own use. The Contractor is not obligated to provide additional temporary works or access for the specific use of others, unless specifically stated in the Contract. However, he may agree to do so for additional payment.

4.7 Setting Out

The setting out data may be provided directly by the Employer to the Contractor, but is more commonly provided by the Engineer on behalf of the Employer. A formal hand-over of beacons and other survey points, including a physical examination, is recommended in order to avoid later disputes concerning their existence.

The Contractor is responsible for setting out the Works using the provided data and shall notify the Engineer of any errors observed during the setting out operation. If the Contractor incurs additional cost or is delayed as a consequence of incorrect data, he is entitled to an extension of time for any delay together with payment of his additional costs plus reasonable profit.

In addition to a timely notification of his claim, the Contractor is strongly advised to maintain accurate records (preferably in co-operation with the Engineer) of the delays and additional costs incurred.

'*Thereafter the Engineer is required to proceed in accordance with Sub-Clause 3.5 and to agree or determine to what extent the error could not reasonably have been discovered*' and to evaluate the Contractor's entitlement to additional payment and/or an extension of time.

4.8 Safety Procedures

The detail and implementation of safety regulations vary markedly from country to country. The more developed the country of execution, the more detailed are the laws relating to safety requirements likely to be. The laws of the country of execution of the Works will prevail over any obligation given in the Contract.

Due to this diversity in law and application, FIDIC can only address the issue of safety in a generalised manner.

Most major contractors working in the field of international construction will have available their own in-house safety manual. Therefore a check must be made to make sure this manual conforms to local legal requirements and fully address the requirements of the Contract.

Therefore it is recommended that a further document be prepared to supplement the Contractor's Standard Safety Manual. This would also take into account local language and local customs requirements.

The two documents taken together can be considered analogous to the FIDIC General Conditions and Particular Conditions of Contract. Although not identified in the FIDIC standard forms, most contract documents require the appointment of a Safety Officer whose duty is to oversee safety issues. The Safety Officer should report directly to the Contractor's Representative.

The Employer and the Engineer, because of their physical presence on site, also have an important contribution to make to site safety.

4.9 Quality Assurance

'*The Contractor is required to institute a quality assurance system to demonstrate compliance with the requirements of the Contract.*' Many contractors working in the field of international construction will have a standard in-house manual conforming to the requirements of the international standard ISO 9001. If the contract documents do not refer to ISO 9001, the Contractor may choose to confirm his intentions to comply with ISO 9001 as part of his tender submittal. Each contract will have its own particular requirements and the Contractor will need to prepare supplementary documents to demonstrate conformity with those particular requirements. These documents have to be submitted to the Engineer for 'information'(not approval) at each stage of the Contract.

The Engineer is authorised to audit any aspect of the quality assurance system. Before submitting documentation to the Engineer, the Contractor is required to approve the documentation himself. ISO 9001 is not yet a standard document in use in all countries. However, the Contractor may still find it convenient to base his proposals on ISO 9001.

4.10 Site Data

The Engineer has no responsibility in respect of the data supplied by the Employer to all tenderers. Should the Employer supply additional data to the Contractor after award of contract, the Engineer would doubtlessly wish to be fully informed and provided with copies of the data, as it may be significant in the Engineer's consideration of any claims made by the Contractor under Sub-Clause 4.12, Unforeseeable Physical Conditions. Also refer to Chapter 1, Sub-Clause 4.10 of this book.

4.11 Sufficiency of the Accepted Contract Amount

The contents of this sub-clause does not require any action from the Engineer.

4.12 Unforeseeable Physical Conditions

If the Contractor encounters physical conditions which he considers to have been 'unforeseeable', he shall give notice to the Engineer, with a copy to the Employer, and shall be entitled to an extension of time and payment of any cost arising as a consequence of the unforeseeable physical conditions.

'Unforeseeable' is defined in Sub-Clause 1.1.6.8 as meaning *'not reasonably foreseeable by an experienced contractor by the date for submission of the Tender'*. It will be noted that the definition given refers to a hypothetical experienced contractor and not to the Contractor himself. In the presentation of any claim under this heading, the Contractor's logic should be to demonstrate that a typical experienced contractor could not have foreseen the unforeseeable condition and therefore he, the Contractor, also an experienced contractor, would equally not have foreseen the unforeseeable condition. What the Contractor himself may or may not have foreseen is not of immediate concern. Frequently, secondary disputes may arise over the practical application of the word 'reasonably'. In attempting to provide guidance on this point, the FIDIC Contracts Guide expresses the opinion that for a contract of three years duration, an experienced contractor might be expected to foresee an event which occurs on average once every six years. An event which occurs once every 10 years might be regarded as 'unforeseeable'. Another authority has commented that the reference is to what was reasonably foreseeable by an experienced contractor and not by a university academic.

Secondly, the cut-off date for foreseeability is the date of tender and not the Base Date. This criterion appears to be harsh on the Contractor, since it implies that he has to conduct one last site inspection just before submitting his tender offer, which is likely to be impractical.

FIDIC defines physical conditions *'as natural physical conditions and man made or other physical conditions and pollutants which the Contractor encounters at the Site, including sub-surface and hydrological conditions, but excluding climatic conditions.*

"Sub-surface conditions" are those conditions below the surface, including those with a body of water and those below the river bed or sea bed.

"Hydrological conditions" means the flows of water, including those which are attributable to off-Site climatic conditions.

"Physical conditions" excludes climatic conditions at the Site and therefore excludes the hydrological consequences of climatic conditions at Site.'

The foregoing leads to the following basic procedure in dealing with claims under Clause 4.12, Unforeseeable Physical Conditions.

- In the preparation of his claim submittal, the Contractor must first demonstrate unforeseeability (by an experienced contractor), with

particular reference to Sub-Clause 4.10 'Site Data' and any other data which may be contained elsewhere in the Contract Documents.
- The unforeseeable condition must be encountered at the Site. Unforeseeable conditions off-site do not meet this criterion.
- The unforeseeable condition must be physical and not concerned with administrative events for example.
- Adverse '*climatic conditions on the Site, such as the effect of rainfall*', wind or abnormal temperatures are excluded. However, it will be noted that Sub-Clause 17.3 (item h) identifies as an Employer's Risk '*any operation of the forces of nature which is unforeseeable or against which an experienced contractor could not reasonably have been expected to have taken adequate preventative precautions*'. (Sub-Clause 17.4 describes the of the Contractor in respect of an Employer's Risk event.)
- Adverse hydrological conditions, such as flows of water, are admissible including those attributable to off-site conditions, such as flooding from a nearby stream or river.

A significant portion of claims submitted under this sub-clause relate to sub-surface geological conditions, which may require expert opinion in support of the claim. Claims relating to adverse hydrological conditions require an evaluation of the statistical frequency and severity of the unforeseeable event and a demonstration that the frequency and/or severity of the event was not foreseeable by an experienced contractor. This type of unforeseeable event may be covered by some part of the contract insurances, but it should be borne in mind that insurers do not award extensions of time.

Certain extreme categories of natural disasters which could also not been foreseen by an experienced contractor are included in Sub-Clause 19.1 'Definition of Force Majeure'.

Should the Contractor consider he has encountered an unforeseen physical condition, he is required to give notice to the Engineer in accordance with the 28 day period stated in Sub-Clause 20.1. Excepting in the most obvious circumstances, it is highly likely that there will be a significant time lapse before the existence of the unforeseen physical condition is recognised by the Engineer (and behind the scenes by the Employer).

The Contractor has a duty to continue with the Works regardless of his claim that he has encountered an unforeseen physical condition.

The FIDIC Contracts Guide states that the Contractor '*is expected to use his expertise*' to overcome the adverse conditions. The Engineer should co-operate with the Contractor to identify technical solutions which fulfil the principles of the Engineer's design. This co-operation is important because remedial varied or changes to the performance of the Works may in themselves represent Variations and Adjustments as described in Clause 13.

Should the Engineer for whatever reason decline to participate in the process to find solutions, the Contractor may have to proceed unilaterally. In such cases it is vital that the Contractor keeps the Engineer informed of the Contractor's proposals which should be supported by adequate technical documentation.

In dealing with the perceived unforeseen physical condition, the Contractor must maintain detailed records of his activities on a day by day basis to the

Engineer for agreement. The Engineer may decline to agree these records as a basis for payment, but he may be prepared to agree them for 'record purposes only' without any contractual commitment. It would be most unfortunate if there was no response from the Engineer to agree detailed records, as the Contractor would be fully entitled to evaluate any future claim based on those records. DAB and Arbitration boards may take a negative view of non co-operation.

In the event of a valid claim for unforeseen physical conditions, Sub-Clause 4.12, the Contractor is entitled to payment of (additional) costs incurred as a consequence of overcoming the unforeseen physical condition.

The Contractor is theoretically entitled to payment for the original executed work at the billed rates (or varied rates) and in addition payment of the Cost of any additional measures necessary to deal with the unforeseen physical condition. Payments at bill rates include a profit allowance, whereas payment of Cost excludes profit.

In practice it may be difficult, if not impractical, for the Contractor to divide the total package of work executed by him solely on the basis of Cost. He would then lose the profit element on the original work component. In preparing his records, the Contractor should consider the possibility of separating out the two components. Again this is a topic that could be usefully discussed in advance with the Engineer.

FIDIC has introduced an additional proviso not contained in previous standard contract forms concerning more favourable conditions. Before any additional cost is finally agreed or determined, the Engineer may (permissively) review whether other physical conditions in similar parts of the Works (if any) were more favourable than could reasonably be foreseen when the Contractor submitted the Tender. It may be presumed that the foreseeability criterion applies to that which could be foreseen by an experienced contractor and does not refer to what the Engineer considers foreseeable.

The above is most likely to apply to projects involving repetitive work – building foundations, machine bases and similar. Should the Engineer determine that the Contractor has received a benefit as a consequence of more favourable conditions, then the cost due elsewhere to the Contractor for proven unforeseeable physical conditions shall be reduced accordingly.

Finally, the Engineer in making his determination, may take account of the physical conditions actually foreseen by the Contractor when submitting the Tender. The FIDIC Contracts Guide notes that if a dispute arises and is referred to the DAB or to arbitration, the members may wish to view evidence of the Contractor's assumptions, query the authors and query why this evidence was not provided to the Engineer at an earlier date.

4.13 Rights of Way and Facilities

Occasionally it may happen that the Contractor requires other rights of access to the Site in addition to those provided by the Employer under the terms of the Contract. The Contractor has the obligation to obtain such rights of way at his own risk and cost.

In addition, the Contractor may wish to occupy areas not within the Site and not otherwise within areas to be provided by the Employer under the terms of the Contract. Again the Contractor has the duty to obtain use of these areas at his own risk and cost.

4.14 Avoidance of Interference

The Contractor has a general obligation not to *'interfere unnecessarily or improperly with the convenience of the public, access and footpaths'*.

If interference is an unavoidable consequence of the design, this ideally should be identified in the Contract Documents, so that appropriate arrangements can be put in place before any work is carried out.

The Contractor should adopt appropriate arrangements and methods in order that claims from third parties are minimised. Such arrangements are subject to the consent of the Engineer and will likely require discussion with the affected parties. However, it is to be noted that Sub-Clause 18.3(d)(ii) states that insurances may exclude *'damage which is an unavoidable result of the Contractor's obligations to execute the Works and remedy any defects…'*. In such circumstances third party claims are an Employer's risk event.

4.15 Access Routes

In the preparation of the Tender, the Contractor has the obligation to satisfy himself *'as to the suitability and availability of access routes to the Site and other work areas'*.

Many public authorities have strict rules concerning the use by the Contractor of roads falling under their authority and the Contractor's requirements may have to be negotiated in some detail. The Contractor may be required to contribute to road protection measures or maintenance costs. Early clarification is needed since the estimated cost of any such measures has to be included in the Tender offer. This would be an appropriate topic for discussion in any pre-tender site inspection.

4.16 Transport of Goods

'The Contractor is to give the Engineer no less than 21 days notice of the date arrival of Plant and major items of Goods on Site.' Further the Contractor is responsible for all aspects of Goods arriving on Site.

It is assumed that the Contractor will have prepared a full schedule of the intended arrival date on Site of his Plant and major items of Goods. These schedules could be periodically updated with arrival dates shown for presentation to the Engineer. All Contractor's Plant and Goods are to be insured for their on-site value.

4.17 Contractor's Equipment

All Contractor's Equipment when brought on Site *'shall be deemed to be exclusively intended for the execution of the Works'*. Major items shall not be removed from Site without the permission of the Engineer.

Since Contractor's Equipment also includes Subcontractor's Equipment an appropriate reference is to be included in the Subcontract Documents. It should be clarified if hire trucks and hire cars in use on the Works are excluded from this requirement.

4.18 Protection of Environment

The general obligations of the Contractor are given in this sub-clause and are likely to be amplified by specific requirements identified by the Employer elsewhere in the Contract Documents.

The Contractor is required *'to take all reasonable steps to protect the environment (both on and off the Site) and to limit damage, nuisance and pollution'*. Increasingly, governments and local agencies have legal authority to ensure the protection of the environment by the Contractor and his subcontractors and suppliers. Specific requirements may include controlled disposal of inert waste construction materials such as concrete, asphalt, rubble, etc. Toxic materials such as waste oil and paint will require special disposal provisions. Domestic and office waste may be recyclable, otherwise permission to burn combustible waste may be required. Fees or charges may be imposed by the competent authorities. Should the Contractor provide living accommodation, the disposal of treated waste water and sewage is likely to be strictly controlled. All these requirements have a cost implication to be evaluated by the Contractor for inclusion in the tender. The Engineer will require method statements from the Contractor to explain how he will fulfil his contractual obligations.

4.19 Electricity, Water, Gas

Other than provided in the Contract, the Contractor is *'responsible for the supply of the above services at his own risk and expense'*.

If Employer-provided services are already available at or near the site, the Contractor may be required to provide metering devices. Normally, if the Employer is to provide these services and the Site has a potentially high demand, it is necessary that the Parties liaise together to ensure the services are available, of sufficient capacity and not subject to shortages or other factors which could cause delays to the Works. This is particularly important if more than one contractor is taking supplies; the supply of electricity at peak times may exceed the Employer's ability to provide those supplies.

4.20 Employer's Equipment and Free-Issue Material

It may be that the Employer has available equipment and materials which he wishes the Contractor to utilise on the Works. As a general rule, it is not compulsory for the Contractor to use the Employer's Equipment and Free-Issue Materials. Frequently the potential use of these items is included by means of optional bill items in order to reduce the Tender Price if at all possible.

The Contract Documents will provide full details of the Employer's Equipment and Free-Issue Material.

If it is agreed that the Contractor shall use the Employer's Equipment and Free-Issue Materials in the execution of the Works, then the following basic procedures follow:

(a) The Contractor shall visually inspect the Employer's Equipment and Free-Issue Materials at the Employer's storage location and shall give notice to the Engineer of any shortages, visible defects and faults.
(b) The Employer shall make good the shortages and defects.
(c) After rectification, the Employer's Equipment and Free-Issue Materials shall come under the care and custody of the Contractor. This does not relieve the Employer for any shortage, defects and faults not apparent from a visual inspection. The Contractor should ensure that all items are covered by his insurances.

4.21 Progress Reports

It has long been a requirement of most contracts that the Contractor prepares monthly progress reports for submittal to the Engineer.

By this sub-clause FIDIC has introduced formality and structure to this reporting system. Of particular importance to the Contractor is the cross-reference contained in Sub-Clause 14.3, wherein it is stated that an Application for Interim Payment Certificates by the Contractor shall (as part of the supporting documentation) include a progress report for the same period to which the Interim Payment Application refers. Thus any delay in providing the progress report may damage the Contractor's interests. The Contractor therefore should ensure that the progress report is efficiently prepared and submitted to the Engineer in time.

Sub-Clause 4.21 indentifies eight topics to be addressed in the progress report, although it is quite possible that other topics may have to be added to meet the special features of individual projects. It is stated that each report shall cover the following topics:

(a) '*Charts and detailed description of progress*' (including subcontractors). This will focus on the Contractor's progress measured against programmes (see also (h) below)
(b) Photographs
(c) The status of the manufacture of the main items of Plant and Materials
(d) Records of Contractor's Personnel and Equipment (Sub-Clause 6.10)

(e) '*Copies of quality assurance documents, test results and certificates of Materials.*' It may be more convenient to supply bulk documents under separate cover and include only summaries in the report
(f) '*List of notices under Sub-Clause 2.5 (Employer) and notices under Sub-Clause 20.1 (Contractor)*'
(g) '*Safety Statistics*'
(h) '*Comparisons of actual vs planned progress*'. Details of delay events and measures to be taken to overcome the delay
(i) Other.

The Contractor may take the opportunity to highlight other topics which are not included in the above.

Due to the limited time window available for the collection of data and the compilation of reports, it is important that the Contractor uses pro-forma model documents to the maximum extent possible. In this respect it is recommended that the Contractor presents his proposals for the format and content of the reports to the Engineer for discussion at an early stage of the Contract in order that progress reports are prepared in an acceptable manner from the outset.

The Contractor's Representative will need to distribute responsibility for the preparation of various elements of the reports to the appropriate members of his staff. Further, he will need to nominate a suitable person to collate, edit and complete the final preparation of the progress reports. Finally, he should be willing to use his full authority to ensure that the nominated staff complete their given tasks according to a pre-set time schedule.

The Contractor is required to present progress reports until he has completed all work known to be outstanding at the completion date stated in the Taking-Over Certificate.

4.22 Security of Site

This clause requires that the Contractor keeps authorised persons off the Site. Authorised persons are limited to the Contractor's Personnel and any other personnel notified to the Contractor by the Employer or the Engineer including authorised personnel of the Employer's other contractors on the Site (if any).

In addition, although not stated in this sub-clause, the Contractor necessarily may need to safeguard his assets both on and off the Site, including office and accommodation areas. There is no specific statement that the Contractor has to safeguard the assets of the Employer or Engineer (or their staff) on the Site. Nonetheless, good security is of benefit to the Site and the companies employed there and a pragmatic approach to the security of all is recommended.

There may also be insurance issues to be considered.

The preparation of a security plan by the Contractor should be presented to the Employer and the Engineer for their assent. This plan would include the need for site passes and general control of property and personnel, together with detailed action plans in case of emergency.

4.23 Contractor's Operations on Site

The Contractor is required to *'confine his operations to the Site and any additional work areas'* which may be agreed. This requirement extends to the Contractor's Equipment and Personnel. The Contractor is required to keep the Site free from obstructions and remove from Site any rubbish and unwanted items. Upon the issue of a Taking-Over Certificate, *'the Contractor is required to leave the Site and the Works in clean, safe condition'*. Approved spoil areas operating according to the laws of the country may be required. The Contractor may incur charges as a consequence. Cross-reference should also be made to Sub-Clause 4.18 'Protection of the Environment'.

4.24 Fossils

Although headed 'Fossils', this sub-clause also refers to coins, articles of value or antiquity and other items of geological or archaeological interest. Upon discovering any of the above, *'the Contractor shall give notice'* (recommended verbal notice followed by written notice) *'to the Engineer'*, with a copy to the Employer.

The Engineer shall give instructions to the Contractor how to proceed with the Works which would include any necessary measures. If it is anticipated that antiquities are likely to be encountered on the Site, it would be helpful if written procedures were made available in advance by the appropriate authorities in order to minimise any delays to the Works.

Should the Contractor consider that he will be delayed or otherwise incur additional costs, he should promptly give written notice of claim with reference to this sub-clause and Sub-Clause 20.1.

The FIDIC Contracts Guide comments that *'this sub-clause makes no reference to the finding of fossils having to be unforeseeable because the Contract should specify the procedure in respect of foreseeable findings'*.

The Contractor should be alerted to any requirements of the local law.

Clause 5 Nominated Subcontractors

5.0 Nominated Subcontractors – General

The FIDIC Contracts Guide contains a number of valuable comments on the merits or otherwise of the engagement of nominated Subcontractors. Commentary is provided to assist the Employer or Engineer in making decisions whether part or parts of the Works shall be executed by nominated Subcontractors.

Firstly the Guide cautions that it may be preferable to use means other than nominated Subcontractors to engage specialist subcontractors or suppliers in the execution of some parts of the Works:

- the Contract may make specific reference to the manufacturer without making him a nominated Subcontractor
- should the Employer wish to ensure that a part of the Works is executed by a specialist company and not by the Contractor himself, a listing of the chosen specialists may be included in the Specification and tenderers invited to specify their chosen Subcontractor
- if the Employer wishes to ensure that part of the project is designed by a specialist company (and this may be linked to the supply of preferred materials or plant), a separate contract may be more manageable and therefore preferred.

The principal advantage of nominated Subcontractors include the possibility of the Employer participating in the choice of nominated Subcontractors. In addition the Employer does not need to become involved in the coordination problems between Contractor and the nominated Subcontractor.

The Employer and Engineer should not deal directly with a nominated Subcontractor, as such interference may impinge on the Contractor's general responsibility for the defaults of the nominated Subcontractor as stated in Sub-Clause 4.4. The Contractor should be requested to identify which members of his staff will directly supervise the activities of any nominated Subcontractors and who can be directly contacted by the Engineer or Employer whenever necessary.

5.1 Definition of 'Nominated Subcontractor'

'In the Contract "nominated Subcontractor" means a subcontractor

(a) *who is stated in the Contract as being a nominated Subcontractor, or*
(b) *whom the Engineer, under Clause 13, Variations and Adjustments, instructs the Contractor to employ as a Subcontractor.*'

(a) If the nominated Subcontractor is to be named in the Contract, then not only should the terms of the proposed subcontract be specified, but also coordination and any other requirements.

(b) The Engineer may, in addition to instructing the appointment of a nominated Subcontractor under Sub-Clause 13.3, Variations, also give similar instructions under Sub-Clause 13.6, Daywork.

5.2 Objection to Nomination

The Contractor has the right to object to the employment of a nominated Subcontractor under specific circumstances. The Contractor must inform the Engineer in writing as soon as practicable with supporting particulars.

A possible resolution of an objection by the Contractor is the provision of an indemnification by the Employer. The Engineer is not authorised to issue any indemnification on behalf of the Employer.

5.3 Payments to Nominated Subcontractors

The Contractor is obliged to pay to the nominated Subcontractor those amounts which the Engineer certifies to be due in accordance with the Contract. Nominated Subcontractors will inevitably prepare their own estimation of the work completed in each period and will require to liaise with the Engineer and Contractor to finalise the amount due for certification. The percentage to be added for the Contractor's overheads and profits will be added in the Interim Payment Application prepared by the Contractor.

Once the Engineer has certified the amounts due to the nominated Subcontractors, the Contractor can then issue a corresponding subcontract Interim Payment Certificate to the nominated Subcontractors.

5.4 Evidence of Payments

Before issuing a Payment Certificate, the Engineer has the right to request the Contractor to provide evidence that the nominated Subcontractor has received all amounts due in accordance with previous Payment Certificates.

Considering the 56 day payment cycle given in Sub-Clause 14.7, Payment, there will be Payment Certificates not yet due for payment to the Contractor and therefore not due for payment to the nominated Subcontractor.

Also it is likely that the Contractor will require additional time from the date he is paid by the Employer in order to make arrangements to pay the nominated Subcontractor (a 7–10 day interval is common).

Clause 6 Staff and Labour

6.5 Working Hours

This sub-clause states that no work shall be carried out on recognised days of rest, or outside the normal working hours stated in the Appendix to Tender. It would be hoped that the stated working hours are compatible with the type of work to be executed by the Contractor.

Reference is made in Chapter 1, Sub-Clause 6.5 to the need for the Employer to evaluate the likely working practices and needs of the Contractor when deciding the working hours permitted for inclusion in the Appendix to Tender.

Some operations may run around the clock; serving and maintenance of plant will take place at unsociable hours, services including power supplies, pumping operations and similar will require constant attendance. Emergency services may also be required. It is recommended that these issues be discussed and arranged between the Parties at a very early stage of the Contract in order that the Engineer can organise his staff appropriately.

6.7 Health and Safety

The Contractor has a general obligation to take all reasonable precautions to maintain the health and safety of the Contractor's Personnel. The exact requirements may be defined in the Contract, but may be expected to be flexible enough to meet changing site circumstances.

The Contractor shall appoint an accident prevention officer at the Site, responsible for maintaining safety and protection against accidents.

The Employer may require the Engineer also to provide his own accident prevention officer to liaise with the Contractor's officer responsible for the Contractor's activities.

6.8 Contractor's Superintendence

The Contractor is obliged to provide adequate superintendence of the execution of the Works. In addition to basic considerations such as numbers of supervisors and their experience, consideration shall be given to their ability to communicate in the language for communications.

6.9 Contractor's Personnel

The Engineer is entitled to request that any personnel employed on the Site or Works by the Contractor who proves inadequate for a number of stated reasons, shall be removed from the Site on the Engineer's request.

6.10 Records of Contractor's Personnel and Equipment

The Contractor shall submit to the Engineer each calendar month full detailed listing of each class of the Contractor's Personnel and Contractor's Equipment on the Site. The Engineer and the Contractor should agree the format of these records which will form part of the Monthly Report to be submitted by the Contractor in accordance with Sub-Clause 4.21(d), Progress Reports.

These records may also be valuable in the evaluation of variations and claims.

Clause 7 Plant, Materials and Workmanship

7.1 Manner of Execution

This sub-clause describes the general obligations of the Contractor in carrying out the manufacture of the Plant, the production and manufacture of Materials and general execution of the Works. The Engineer's duties will include ensuring compliance with these general requirements.

7.2 Samples

The Contractor is required to submit samples of Materials, together with all pertinent data, including details of use or application, to the Engineer for his consent. It will be noted that the Engineer is generally required to consent, and not to approve, the use of Materials whose suitability for inclusion in the Works remains a Contractor's risk.

It is recommended that the submittal of the samples of Materials be rigorously controlled by the use of standard submittal forms, a model of which is described in Appendix G.

7.3 Inspection

The Employer's Personnel (which by reference to Sub-Clause 1.1.2.6 includes the Engineer and his staff) has right of full access to all parts of the Site. Further the Employer's Personnel is entitled to access the production facilities (both on and off site) in order to review the progress of manufacture of Plant and Material. The Contractor is required to provide the Employer's Personnel full opportunity and support to carry out these inspection activities.

Should the Employer's Personnel intend to conduct inspections of off-site production facilities, including facilities in a country other than the country of inspection, then the Contractor shall ensure the facilities are made available for inspection as required. The Contractor is not responsible for any costs incurred by the Employer's Personnel in making these inspections.

For convenience and to avoid high costs, the Employer may find it appropriate to engage the services of a specialist inspection agency to carry out these off-site inspections, particularly if the inspections are to be periodically repeated.

7.4 Testing

The FIDIC Red Book Conditions of Contract requires the Contractor to perform all testing specified in the Contract. (Exceptionally the Employer will perform any testing required in compliance with Clause 12, Tests after Completion.) The Contractor is to provide all Materials, Equipment and Personnel as may be required to carry out the specified testing.

This sub-clause requires the Engineer to give the Contractor 24 hours notice of his intention to attend tests. Should the Engineer fail to attend after having been given notice, then the testing can continue and will then be deemed to have been made in the Engineer's presence. For his part the Contractor shall agree with the Engineer the time and place of the testing.

If the Contractor suffers delay or incurs additional cost as a consequence of a delay for which the Engineer is responsible, then the Contractor, by reference to Sub-Clause 20.1, shall be entitled to claim both an extension of time and any additional costs.

For larger projects requiring continuous testing, and that have their own testing facilities including qualified staff, it is appropriate that the resources of the Engineer and Contractor will be adequately integrated to ensure that all testing and reporting will be carried out in the most expeditious manner possible.

As a general rule, the concerned staff of the Engineer and the Contractor are likely to be in close contact and will make their own arrangements for any tests required without resort to the formality stated in this sub-clause.

The Contractor is required to promptly forward duly certified test reports to the Engineer for his counter-signature. If the Engineer did not attend tests, then he shall be deemed to have accepted the reports as accurate.

It is recommended that the Engineer and the Contractor agree the format of a consolidated report for inclusion in the monthly Progress Report.

7.5 Rejection

If after examination or testing the Plant, Materials or workmanship are defective or otherwise not in accordance with the Contract, then the Engineer may, after giving notice, reject the same. It may be mutually convenient if the reporting system referred to in Sub-Clause 7.4 is used to confirm rejection.

If the Engineer requires re-testing (under the same terms and conditions as previously) and the Plant, Materials or workmanship remain rejected, then the Employer is entitled to claim from the Contractor any additional costs incurred by the Engineer, all subject to the provisions of Sub-Clause 2.5, Employer's Claims.

7.6 Remedial Work

This sub-clause gives the Engineer the general authority to order the removal from Site and replace any Plant and Materials which are not in accordance with the Contract and order the removal and re-execution of any other work which is not in accordance with the requirements of the Contract.

In addition, the Engineer is given the authority to order additional works necessary for the safety of the Works. The Contractor is required to respond without delay, otherwise the Employer can engage others to carry out the work at the Contractor's expense.

7.7 Ownership of Plant and Materials

The determination of ownership is likely to be subject to the laws of the country. Consequently the Engineer will be dependent upon instructions provided by the Employer and/or his legal advisors.

Each item of Plant and Materials is stated to become the property of the Employer when it is delivered to Site. However, suppliers and subcontractors may have provided Plant and Materials on credit and may by the terms of the supply subcontract retain ownership until paid by the Contractor. It is unlikely that the Engineer will have knowledge of the detail of these supply subcontracts and resolution of ownership disputes may take time to achieve.

However, this sub-clause further states that the Plant and Material shall become the property of the Employer when the Contractor is entitled to payment. This requirement is to be included in the subcontract documents. The FIDIC Contracts Guide explains that a change in ownership occurs as soon as the Contractor is entitled under Sub-Clause 8.10 to payment and not when he subsequently receives payment.

Assuming that the Employer is prepared to make payment for the Plant and Materials actually delivered to Site, the Laws of the Country have first to be considered to ensure that payment is made to the correct party.

7.8 Royalties

Should the Contractor intend to take material from off site quarries and other borrow areas, it would be prudent for the Engineer to check into the status of any royalty payments which may become due.

Clause 8 Commencement, Delays and Suspension

8.1 Commencement of Works

The Engineer shall give the Contractor not less than 7 days' notice of the Commencement Date. The Commencement Date is the date on which the Time for Completion commences. Evidently the Employer should not authorise the Engineer to give notice of the Commencement unless he is able to provide the Contractor with right of access to and possession of Site as required by Sub-Clause 2.1.

The Commencement Date shall be within 42 days after the Contractor receives the Letter of Acceptance. As noted in Sub-Clause 1.1.1.3 *'if there is no letter of acceptance, the expression "Letter of Acceptance" means the Contract Agreement and the date of issuing or receiving the Letter of Acceptance means the date of signing the Contract'*.

After receiving the Notice to Commence, the Contractor is required to commence execution of the Works as soon as practicable and to proceed with due expedition.

8.2 Time for Completion

This sub-clause describes the fundamental obligation of the Contractor to complete the whole of the Works within the Time for Completion.

8.3 Programme

The Contractor is required to submit a detailed time programme to the Engineer within 28 days after receiving the notice to commence the Works.

The Employer may have provided an outline programme with the Tender Documents which demonstrates the general practicability of constructing the Works within the stated Time for Completion. As part of his tender presentation, the Contractor will be expected to confirm this tender programme or alternatively to produce his own intended programme of Works. This tender programme will then form part of the Contract Documents.

Considering that the Contractor will probably have advance knowledge that his tender has been successful, it is appropriate that the Contractor commences with the preparation of a Programme of Works conforming to the detailed requirements of this sub-clause as soon as possible.

There is an overriding need for an accurate, realistic programme which, in addition to conforming to the general requirements of the Contract, is sufficiently detailed to facilitate periodic monitoring and the evaluation of the consequences of delays whatever the cause of those delays.

The Engineer has an important role to play in the preparation of the Programme and will need to examine the Programme in detail and be satisfied that critical and near critical activities are identified together with potential 'pinch' points that need careful monitoring if delays are to be avoided. In order to avoid over-cluttering of the presentation of the programme, these activities could be separately listed. The Contractor should be requested to list the resources which are to be provided in order to achieve the Programme so that the Engineer can make an assessment of the likely consequences of delays or additional works on the Time for Completion.

Following submittal of the Programme by the Contractor, the Engineer has 21 days to give notice of the extent to which it does not comply with the requirements. There is no specific requirement for the Engineer to formally approve the Contractor's programme. In the absence of comment from the Engineer, the Contractor shall proceed in accordance with the submitted Programme.

The Contractor is required to promptly give notice to the Engineer when he becomes aware of specific events or circumstances which '*may adversely affect the work, increase the Contract Price or delay the execution of the Works*'. The FIDIC Contracts Guide explains '*that the obligation to notify includes events other than those listed in Sub-Clause 8.4*'.

The Engineer may give notice to the Contractor that a programme is no longer consistent with actual progress and/or the Contractor's stated intentions and therefore requires revision.

8.4 Extension of Time

Provided that the Contractor has complied with the requirements of Sub-Clause 20.1, the Engineer is required to determine (refer to Sub-Clause 3.5) or agree the Extension of Time for Completion and any additional payment due to the Contractor. Any analysis of the Contractor's entitlements can vary in complexity according to the nature of the claim. Analysis will be in part dependent on the quality of the programme of work (refer to Sub-Clause 8.3) and a financial evaluation will depend on the maintenance of detailed records of the relevant delay events and their aftermath.

Ultimately the Employer may incur both direct costs and consequential losses because the Works are delivered late. Close cooperation between Employer and Engineer are self-evidently important if this process is to be managed efficiently.

8.5 Delay Caused by Authorities

Three conditions apply to delays caused by public authorities:

- The Contractor is required to have followed procedures set out by the authority. The Contractor would need to obtain copies of the procedures in order to demonstrate his compliance. However, frequently the written procedures are not readily available and verbal directives will need to be recorded.
- These authorities delay or disrupt the Contractor's work. Proof of delay and disruption would depend on detailed record keeping by the Contractor, supported by appropriate letters recording events as they occur.

- The delay or disruption must be unforeseeable. 'Unforeseeable' is defined in Sub-Clause 1.1.6.8 as *'not reasonably foreseeable by an experienced Contractor at the date of tender'*. It is not possible to predict what might be regarded as unforeseeable. Further commentary on the interpretation of unforeseeable is provided in the discussion in Chapter 1, Sub-Clause 8.5, Unforeseeable Physical Conditions.

8.6 Rate of Progress

If progress is too slow for the Contractor to complete the Works within the Time for Completion and/or progress has fallen behind the current programme, then the Engineer may instruct the Contractor to submit a revised programme (reference Sub-Clause 8.3, Programme) together with a supporting report describing the revised methods which the Contractor proposes to adopt in order to expedite progress and complete within the Time for Completion.

For this sub-clause to be applicable, it requires that the cause(s) of delay is(are) other than those listed in Sub-Clause 8.4, Extension of Time for Completion.

The Contractor may have a number of outstanding requests for extensions of time still requiring a determination by the Engineer. The danger is that failure to deal expeditiously with the Contractor's requests for extension of time could lead to a situation where there was no longer any Time for Completion. Time is said to be *'at large'*. These difficulties can be compounded if the Engineer requires the authority of the Engineer to permit the award of an extension of time and permission is not given within a reasonable time.

The Engineer may decide that the Contractor is entitled to only a part of the total extension of time requested by the Contractor or may decide to issue an interim extension of time pending further review. The amount of additional time authorised on an interim basis cannot be reduced in any future award.

It is quite possible that the Contractor will not be able to complete within the Time for Completion and yet has no valid grounds for the award of an extension of time. In these circumstances it may be preferable to have a realistic working programme to be used for control purposes with clear objectives rather than an unworkable programme which does not reflect actual site activities. The status of the programme in use for control but not in compliance with the requirements of the Contract should be formally recorded because the implication is that the Contractor is inevitably going to be liable to the imposition of delay damages.

8.7 Delay Damages

If the Contractor fails to complete within the Time for Completion, then the Employer, subject to Sub-Clause 2.5, shall be entitled to payment of delay damages. The delay damages shall be the sum stated in Appendix to Tender.

It will be noted that this is a claim to be presented by the Employer and not the Engineer.

8.8 Suspension of Work

This sub-clause gives the Engineer the authority to suspend all or part of the Works. During the execution of the Works, circumstances may arise which result in the Works having to be suspended. The causes of the suspension can be divided into four categories:

(a) Suspension necessary to meet the additional or changed requirements of the Employer. Examples could include the need for a major change in design, political considerations, financial limitations, etc.
(b) Suspension as a consequence of improper practices by the Contractor or his subcontractors. For example safety concerns or the aftermath of an accident may result in suspension ordered by the Engineer or a government authority.
(c) Suspension resulting from an event for which neither Party is responsible. These causes are addressed in detail in Clause 19 'Force Majeure', which provides details of the Contractor's obligations and entitlements.
(d) Suspension arising from natural causes which are not Force Majeure. A major flood may automatically suspend the progress of the Works.

The expectation is that the Engineer would instruct a suspension of work in respect of category (a) and possible category (b) above. Evidently there is no value in the Engineer issuing a formal suspension order in respect of categories (c) and (d).

Following receipt of a suspension instruction, the Contractor has a general duty '*to protect, store and secure the Works*'.

If the reason for the suspension arises from the Contractor's risk event, then the provisions of the following Sub-Clauses 8.9, 8.10 and 8.11 do not apply.

8.9 Consequences of Suspension

For all events causing a suspension of the Works, the Contractor must keep detailed records of all his activities and costs, since for the majority of causes the Contractor will be entitled to claim reimbursement from the Employer or from his own insurers.

It is particularly important that detailed records be maintained of idle resources. A lengthy suspension may require a run down of manpower. The consequences should be discussed with the Employer and Contractor before their implementation.

This sub-clause states that '*if the Contractor suffers delay or incurs cost from complying with the Engineer's instructions, he shall give notice to the Engineer and shall be entitled*' (subject to compliance with Sub-Clause 20.1) to an extension of time (refer to Sub-Clause 8.4) and to payment of his costs. It is to be noted that this entitlement is conditional on the Engineer issuing instructions. Since it is unlikely that a Contractor would unilaterally suspend the Works for a category (a) cause listed in the above commentary for Sub-Clause 8.8, as a consequence the Engineer would be obligated to issue an appropriate instruction.

The sub-clause concludes by stating that *'the Contractor shall not be entitled to an extension of time or payment of the cost incurred in making good faulty work or for any failure to protect, store or secure in accordance with Sub-Clause 8.8'*.

8.10 Payment for Plant and Materials in Event of Suspension

'For a suspension which is not due to any failure on the part of the Contractor he is entitled to payment for any suspended Plant and Materials 28 days after the date of suspension if he takes necessary actions to make the Plant and Materials the property of the Employer'.

Inevitably this process would have to be discussed and formalised with the Employer. It is important to establish ownership of the Plant and Materials as a pre-condition of any payment to the Contractor. Ownership may be subject to the Laws of the Country. The process is optional for the Contractor and may be varied should the cause of suspension be related to financial issues. Payment of any entitlement would be under Clause 14 'Contract Price and Payment'.

8.11 Prolonged Suspension

'If the suspension under Sub-Clause 8.8 has continued for more than 84 days, the Contractor may request the Engineer for permission to proceed. If the Engineer does not give permission within a further period of 28 days, the Contractor may, by giving notice to the Engineer, treat the suspension as an omission under Clause 13 "Variation and Adjustments". If the suspension affects the whole of the Works, the Contractor may give notice of termination under Sub-Clause 16.2.'

In an extreme situation a period of 112 days could elapse before the Contractor is advised whether the Works are to continue or if the period of suspension is to be extended by agreement or if the Works are to be terminated. The Contractor is placed at considerable commercial risk by any suspension and the uncertainty arising from an extended suspension amplifies those risks.

It is important for the Contractor to maintain close contact with the Employer and the Engineer in order to obtain an agreement concerning the future of the Contractor's resources both on and off site. Good record keeping by the Contractor is essential to support any claims subsequently presented by him.

8.12 Resumption of Work

'After the permission or instruction to proceed is given, the Contractor and the Engineer shall jointly examine the Works and the Plant and Materials affected by the suspension. The Contractor shall make good any

deterioration or defect which has occurred during the suspension and is entitled to claim his costs under Sub-Clause 8.9 "Consequences of Suspension".'

It is quite possible that the suspension may have disrupted the Contractor's activities in other ways. Personnel may have left the Site and have to be recalled or new Personnel recruited. The Contractor's Equipment may have been stored and requires full servicing before being returned to service. It is very likely that some time will elapse before the Contractor reaches the productivity levels obtained before the suspension.

Any submittal made under Sub-Clause 8.9 should include any cost of disruption and requests for extension of time should include for any effective time loss due to the disruption.

Clause 9 Tests on Completion

9.0 General

The FIDIC Contracts Guide states that *'The Tests on Completion are the tests required by the Engineer in order to determine if the Works (or Section if any) have reached the stage at which the Employer should take over the Works (or Section)'* and *'Tests on Completion must be specified in detail in the Contract'*.

In many former socialist countries the taking over procedures are governed by the Law of the Country and are not subject to the procedures described in Sub-Clauses 10.1 or 10.2. Nonetheless, the satisfactory completion of the Tests on Completion does provide evidence that the Works have been completed, even if this does not itself directly lead to the issue of a Taking-Over Certificate by the Engineer.

9.1 Contractor's Obligations

The term 'Tests on Completion' is defined in Sub-Clause 1.1.3.4 as *'the tests which are specified in the Contract or agreed by both Parties or instructed as a Variation… which are to be carried out before the Works or a Section are taken over by the Employer'*.

The great majority of tests will be performed as the Works proceed, but certain types of testing can only be performed when the Works are nearing completion; an example would be full load tests on electrical systems. This sub-clause covers the possibility that certain specified tests may require an input from the Employer or service providers. Further, it is possible that some tests have to be satisfactorily performed to comply with the requirements of the local authorities or service providers and will require their attendance. Security equipment may also require full-scale testing to be completed before taking over.

The taking over of the Works as described in Sub-Clause 10.1 allows for the possible existence of *'minor outstanding works and defects…'* at the date of taking over which are to be completed in the Defects Notification Period. In some countries *'minor'* is strictly interpreted, so that the amount of outstanding work is very minor indeed.

It is important that the Contractor ascertains the precise level of completion, including the extent of Tests on Completion required for taking over by the Employer well in advance of the projected date of taking over.

This sub-clause requires the Contractor to give to the Engineer not less than 21 days notice of dates for the performance of Tests on Completion.

9.2 Delayed Tests

Should Tests on Completion be delayed by the Employer (reference Sub-Clause 7.4, fifth paragraph, and Sub-Clause 10.3), the Contractor is entitled to claim an extension of time and additional costs.

Alternatively, should the Contractor fail to carry out Tests on Completion, the Engineer may give notice to the Contractor to carry out the tests within a period of 21 days, otherwise the Employer's Personnel may proceed with the tests at the risk and cost of the Contractor. In practice the Employer's Personnel may be reluctant to unilaterally perform Tests on Completion, particularly if they are not familiar with the subject of the tests and are concerned that damage may be caused by their actions.

9.3   Re-testing

The Contractor is required to repeat any failed Tests on Completion. Any remedial works undertaken may affect other Tests on Completion.

Thereafter, should the defects persist and the Works continue to have a reduced value, the Employer may require the Engineer to agree or determine a reasonable deduction in the Contract Price (refer also to Sub-Clause 11.4), as a pre-condition to the issue of a Taking-Over Certificate by the Engineer.

Clause 10 Employer's Taking Over

10.0 General

The reader is reminded that in many countries the taking over procedures are governed by the Law of the Country and are not subject to the provisions of Sub-Clauses 10.1 and 10.2.

10.1 Taking Over of the Works and Sections

The Works shall be taken over by the Employer when (i) the Works have been completed in accordance with the Contract and (ii) a Taking-Over Certificate has been issued by the Engineer.

The Works can be taken over in Sections, provided that there is a specific provision in the Contract defining those Sections, otherwise the Works are to be taken over at one time in their entirety.

The Contractor shall apply to the Engineer (copy to the Employer) for a Taking-Over Certificate to be issued not earlier than 14 days before the Works or Sections will, in the opinion of the Contractor, be ready for taking over. On receiving the Contractor's application, the Engineer shall, within a period of 28 days, issue the Taking-Over Certificate, provided that he agrees that the Works or Section are substantially complete, excepting for minor outstanding works and minor defects which do not substantially affect the use of the taken-over Works or Section by the Employer.

The degree of completeness required is not precisely defined. Typically it may be anticipated that secure areas (such as airport airside areas) and areas that will become inaccessible after taking over will require a high level of completeness. In contrast, for a rural highway a lower standard of completion may be acceptable for taking over purposes.

As the Works approach completion, it is a useful practice for the Engineer and Contractor to jointly make informal inspections of the Works in advance of any formal application by the Contractor for a Taking-Over Certificate. Outstanding works and defects can be dealt with expeditiously and, as a consequence, the eventual listing of outstanding works and defects can be minimised.

The Contractor will be well aware that if his request for a Taking-Over Certificate is rejected by the Engineer for valid reasons, he faces a delay of at least 28 days before a second application for a Taking-Over Certificate has to be again evaluated by the Engineer.

The Employer has no right to use the Works, if the Contractor has failed to complete the Works in accordance with the Contract, which effectively means that the Taking-Over Certificate has to be issued before the Works can be used by the Employer.

It may happen that the Employer would prefer to take over parts of the Works, even though there is no provision in the Contract. In such circumstances the Employer has the option to take-over parts of the Works as described in Sub-Clause 10.3.

10.2 Taking Over of Parts of the Works

Circumstances may arise wherein the Employer wishes to take possession of a part of the Works which is not a Section defined in the Contract.

The Engineer may then be authorised by the Employer to issue a Taking-Over Certificate for a part of the Works. The Employer is not authorised to use any part of the Works (unless it is a temporary measure agreed by the Parties), unless and until the Engineer has issued a Taking-Over Certificate.

If it is necessary that the Employer uses a part of the Works before the Taking-Over Certificate is issued, then the part is deemed to have been taken over as from the date on which it is occupied. The Contractor shall be given the opportunity to complete the Works including any Tests on Completion.

If the Contractor incurs Cost as a result of the taking over and use of a part of the Works by the Employer (examples could include the cost of temporary traffic control measures, barriers, temporary access, etc.), then the Contractor shall be entitled to payment of any such Cost plus profit, subject to notice having been given in accordance with Sub-Clause 20.1. It is recommended that any special measures are pre-agreed and evaluated by the Engineer and the Contractor.

10.3 Interference with Tests on Completion

If the Contractor is prevented for more than 14 days from carrying out Tests on Completion from a cause for which the Employer is responsible, then the Employer is deemed to have taken over on the date which the Tests on Completion would otherwise have been completed. The Contractor is required to carry out the Tests on Completion after the issue of the Taking-Over Certificate.

Subject to giving notice under Sub-Clause 20.1, the Contractor is entitled to claim an extension of time and payment of any Cost arising plus reasonable profit.

Clause 11 Defects Liability

11.1 Completion of Outstanding Work and Remedying Defects

The Contractor is obligated to complete any outstanding work stated in the Taking-Over Certificate and to execute all work to remedy defects or damage, as may be notified by the Employer before the expiry of the Defects Notification Period. The Contractor has no obligation in respect of fair wear and tear and damage arising from causes which are the responsibility of the Employer. It is in the interest of both the Employer and the Contractor that the Contractor completes any outstanding work and corrects any defects as soon as possible after the issue of the Taking-Over Certificate and not extend this work over the whole of the Defects Notification Period. Periodic inspections of the completed Works by the Parties are recommended when the defects can be checked and progressively signed off.

11.2 Cost of Remedying Defects

The Contractor is responsible for the cost of completing outstanding works and the remedying of defects which fall under the Contractor's responsibility. Should the Contractor consider that he is not responsible for any part of the remedial work that is instructed by the Employer or Engineer, he is required to follow the claims procedure given in Sub-Clause 20.1.

If the defect or damage is eventually not considered a Contractor's fault, then any instructed work shall be dealt with as a Variation (refer to Sub-Clause 13.3, Variation Procedure).

11.3 Extension of Defects Notification Period

Subject to having given notice in accordance with Sub-Clause 2.5, Employer's Claims, the Employer is entitled to an extension of the Defects Notice Period, if and to the extent that the Works or section or major item of Plant cannot be used for their intended purpose by reason of a defect or damage. The extension shall not exceed two years.

11.4 Failure to Remedy Defects

The options open to the Employer in the event the Contractor fails to remedy defects are described in Chapter 1, Sub-Clause 11.4 of this book.

11.5 Removal of Defective Work

If it is necessary to remove from Site a defective or damaged item for repair, the Employer is required to give his consent in writing. The Engineer does not have the authority to permit removal.

The Employer may request the Contractor to provide an acceptable financial security before allowing the defective item to be taken off site.

11.6 Further Tests

Following the remedying of any defect or damage, the Engineer may instruct the repetition of any of the tests described in the Contract. For major/intricate items of Plant, re-testing and certification under factory conditions may be required.

11.8 Contractor to Search

When instructed by the Engineer, the Contractor shall search for the cause of any defect. Unless the cause of the defect is the responsibility of the Contractor, the Contractor shall be entitled to be reimbursed the cost of the search plus a reasonable profit.

11.9 Performance Certificate

The Engineer shall issue the Performance Certificate once the Contractor has completed all his obligations under the Contract. The Performance Certificate shall be issued within 28 days after the expiry of the latest dates of the Defects Notification periods, provided that the Contractor has supplied all Contractor's Documents, completed and tested the Works and remedied any defects.

The issue of the Performance Certificate constitutes acceptance of the Works.

11.11 Clearance of Site

After receiving the Performance Certificate, the Contractor shall remove all surplus and waste from the Site within a period of 28 days, after which the Employer may arrange for the removal or sale of the same at the Contractor's risk and expense.

Clause 12 Measurement and Evaluation

12.1 Works to be Measured

Whenever the Engineer intends to measure any part of the Works, he shall give reasonable notice to the Contractor, who will attend the measurement and supply any particulars required by the Engineer.

In practice, independent arrangements for measurement are likely to be made between the concerned staff of the Engineer and the Contractor with minimal formality. An important exception is any measurement requested for the purposes of Sub-Clause 15.3, Valuation at Date of Termination. Whilst parts of the Works can be measured directly from drawings, other parts of the Works, particularly excavations and earthworks operations which are to be covered up, require prompt field measurement.

Where measurement is to be obtained from these records, these are to be prepared by the Engineer and agreed by the Contractor. The Contractor shall give notice to the Engineer of any inaccuracies within a period of 14 days, otherwise the Engineer's records are to be accepted as correct.

12.2 Method of Measurement

Unless stated otherwise and not withstanding local practice, measurement shall be made of the net actual quantity.

The method of measurement will typically

- be stated in a preamble to the Bill of Quantities or
- referred to a publication such as the Standard Method of Measurement or
- be included as part of the item description of each item in the Bill of Quantities.

The FIDIC Contracts Guide notes that disputes frequently arise as to whether an additional bill item is required or whether the work is covered by another item in the Bill of Quantities.

A common response is that since no specific bill item is provided, the Contractor must be deemed to have included the relevant costs elsewhere in the Contract.

The FIDIC Contracts Guide offers a more sophisticated and reasoned approach to provide a solution, which is summarised as follows:

- '*if the Bill of Quantities clearly requires that an item of work be measured and yet do not provide an item, then an additional Bill item will be required*
- *if the Bill of Quantities does not require a particular item of work to be measured (and does not arise from a Variation), then measurement does not require the addition of a new Bill item*
- *if the Bill of Quantities does not include principles of measurement for a particular item, and the work was described in the Contract (and did not arise from a Variation)… then measurement in accordance with such principles does not require the addition of a new Bill item.*'

12.3 Evaluation

This sub-clause describes the basic methods of evaluating the work executed using Bill rates. The sub-clause also describes how new rates shall be determined under certain conditions. These fall into two categories:

(a) Changes in Quantities of work executed. The changes have to be significant. There are four conditions which have to be satisfied before this provision is actionable.

- the change in quantity is to be more than 10% of the quantity given in the Bill of Quantities
- the change in quantity multiplied by the billed unit rate for this item has to exceed 0.01% of the Accepted Contract Amount
- the change in quantity must change the Cost per unit quantity by more than 1%
- the item is not to be a 'fixed rate item'

The FIDIC Contracts Guide provides further detailed guidance on the application of these arrangements.

(b) Other

- '*work instructed under Clause 13, Variations*
- *no rate or price fixed in the Contract*
- *no existing specific rate or price is appropriate....*'

New rates shall be derived from other bill rates. If there are no relevant rates in the bill of quantities which can be used directly and/or adjusted, then new rates and prices shall be '*derived from the reasonable Cost of executing the work, together with a reasonable profit*'. The Engineer has the authority to determine provisional rates for the purposes of Interim Payment Certificates.

12.4 Omissions

'*When the omission of any work forms part or all of a Variation, the value of which has not been agreed if*:

- *the Contractor will incur (or has incurred) cost which if the work had not been omitted would be deemed to be covered by a sum forming part of the Accepted Contract Amount*
- *the omission of the work will result in this sum not forming part of the Contract Price*
- *the cost is not deemed to be included in the evaluation of any substituted work*

then the Contractor shall give notice in accordance with Sub-Clause 20.1 and shall be entitled to reimbursement of the unrecovered cost.'

The FIDIC Contracts Guide quotes a simple example – the Contractor bought formwork for an item of work subsequently omitted by Variation. The Contractor would be entitled to recover the direct cost of the formwork plus profit.

Clause 13 Variations and Adjustments

13.0 General

Contractors will assume that any Variation issued by the Engineer has been subject to the prior scrutiny and approval of the Employer.

For many contracts additional wording is now included in the Particular Conditions of Contract which formally state that the Engineer is required to obtain the consent of the Employer before issuing a Variation to the Contractor. Given that often a Financing Agency may also need to scrutinise the Variation, the total approval system can become quite extended. Sub-Clause 13.1 prevents the Contractor from altering or modifying the Permanent Works *unless and until the Engineer instructs and approves a Variation*. For example, in order to execute a Variation, the Contractor may require resources with lengthy delivery times.

A lengthy approval process introduces uncertainty into the process for Variations and has the potential to delay the execution of the Works. This is an unsatisfactory arrangement for both the Contractor and the Engineer and is a frequent cause of frustration and delay.

Consequently it is incumbent on all parties to give priority to the approval system for Variations, so that action can be taken as soon as possible.

13.1 Right to Vary

The Engineer may initiate a Variation at any time prior to the issuing of the Taking-Over Certificate for the Works. This can be achieved by instruction or by a request for the Contractor to submit a proposal.

It may happen that drawings issued to the Contractor for construction purposes can contain requirements which are Variations, but these may not be readily recognised as such. In such instances dialogue between the Engineer and the Contractor will be required to establish whether a change to the drawings does correspond to a Variation under the Contract.

Under the terms of the Contract the Contractor is obliged to execute the Works described or required by the Variation unless there are good reasons why the Contractor cannot obtain the Goods required for the Variation.

Variations may include:

(c) *'changes to the quantities of any item of Work although not all changes constitute a Variation. Example: the final volume of earthworks may not be identical to the billed quantities*
(d) *changes to the quality and other characteristics of any item of work*
(e) *changes to the levels, positions, and/or dimensions of any part of the Works*
(f) *omission of any work, unless it is to be carried out by others*
(g) *any additional work, Plant, Materials or services necessary for the Permanent Works*

(h) *changes to the sequence or timing of the execution of the Works (but not the Time for Completion).'*

13.2 Value Engineering

The Contractor may at any time submit (but is not obliged to do so) to the Engineer a written proposal which, if adopted, will

- *'accelerate completion*
- *reduce cost to the Employer....*
- *improve efficiency or value to the Employer....*
- *otherwise be of benefit to the Employer.'*

The proposal shall be prepared and eventually designed by the Contractor at his own expense. Design liability insurance is to be provided by the Contractor and included in the costing of the proposal.

The Contractor may be reluctant to make proposals if there is no financial benefit to him. Since the proposal is made at the Contractor's risk, he may be unwilling to accept the risk of delays to the Works, pending consideration of his proposal by the Engineer (and the Employer). If the proposal reduces cost, then the Contractor is entitled to a fee amounting to 50% of the cost saving. It should also be considered that the adoption of the Contractor's proposal may result in an increase in cost and yet be of benefit to the Employer.

13.3 Variation Procedure

The Engineer is the central figure in the process of administrating Variations.

Initially the Engineer, having formulated the proposed scope of the Variation, will request the Contractor to respond in writing and provide:

(a) a description of the detailed execution of the Variation
(b) its effect on the Programme of Works (Sub-Clause 8.3) and the Time for Completion
(c) a pricing proposal for the evaluation of the Variation in accordance with Clause 12, Measurement and Evaluation.

The Contractor is permitted to make his own proposals for consideration by the Engineer but may be reluctant to do so, particularly if he will incur significant costs (including design costs) which will not be reimbursed if his proposals are not adopted.

13.4 Payment in Applicable Currencies

If the Contract provides for payment in more than one currency and an adjustment is agreed, the amount payable in each currency shall be specified.

The Contract is likely to include a provision that requires payment to the Contractor to be made with fixed percentages of local and foreign currencies.

Generally, payment for work arising from a Variation will be paid with the currency percentages of the Contract. However, there may be occasions when the percentages may require adjustment depending on the source of Goods included in the listing of the Variation. These potential exceptions include:

- payment for some elements of varied works, particularly where their price evaluation is not based on existing bill items (Sub-Clause 13.1)
- payment derived from the process of Value Engineering (Sub-Clause 13.2)
- payments to nominated Subcontractors (Sub-Clause 5.3)
- payments in respect of Provisional Sums (Sub-Clause 13.5)
- payments for dayworks (Sub-Clause 13.6).

13.5   Provisional Sums

Sub-Clause 1.1.4.10 defines a Provisional Sum as '... *a sum which is specified in the Contract as a Provisional Sum, for the execution of any part of the Works or for the supply of Plant, Materials or services under Sub-Clause 13.5*'.

One immediate consequence of this definition is that additional Provisional Sums cannot be introduced after the Contract is formalised and would need to be dealt with under Sub-Clause 13.1.

The Provisional Sum is to be expended in accordance with the Engineer's instructions. It may be used in whole or parts, but the sum provided shall not be exceeded. Further, the Engineer (or Employer) cannot increase the amount of a Provisional Sum.

Typically, Provisional Sums are expended in two areas:

- Work which shall be valued in accordance with the principles and procedures given in Sub-Clause 13.3. Minor incidental works are often for convenience valued as dayworks
- Purchase of Plant, Materials or services to be purchased from a nominated Subcontractor defined in Sub-Clause 5.1 or other suppliers.

It is important that the Engineer specifies the Employer's requirements in detail and if he (or the Employer) has already negotiated prices, full information should be provided to the Contractor.

The Contractor is entitled to be reimbursed the actual amount expended as evidenced by quotations, invoices and similar, together with other direct costs, such as customs charges, agency fees, transport and storage. In addition, the Contractor shall be paid a sum for overhead charges and profit, which is usually given as a percentage of cost. The percentage may be given in a separate schedule or more conventionally in the Appendix to Tender.

Occasionally it may happen that the Contract Documents do not contain specific provision for payment of an on-cost. As a consequence the Engineer may be of the opinion that this omission is to be interpreted as meaning the Contractor is not entitled to any on-cost. This opinion is likely to be disputed by the Contractor. A solution is likely to depend on the circumstances of the omission.

13.6 Daywork

For work of a minor and incidental nature, a Variation is required enabling the work to be executed on a daywork basis and valued in accordance with the Daywork Schedule included in the Contract. FIDIC emphasises that if a Daywork Schedule is not provided, then this sub-clause is of no effect.

The Daywork Schedule will typically consist of hourly rates for Equipment and Labour, together with a price listing for basic materials. More specialised materials can be priced as for Provisional Sums or, if these are site manufactured, appropriate unit rates will need to be negotiated.

The sub-clause is silent on the matter of the cost of time taken to travel to place of execution of the dayworks and unavoidable waiting time. Unless there is specific provision in the Contract to the contrary, it is assumed that the Contractor has entitlement to payment. It is hoped that the Employer will have made his requirements clear at the tender stage in order that the Contractor can make appropriate allowance in his tender.

Daily records shall be maintained by the Contractor and presented to the Engineer for agreement. A sample daily record sheet is provided as Appendix I. These records shall be valued in accordance with the Daywork Schedules and represented for inclusion in the next Interim Payment Application.

13.7 Adjustment for Changes in Legislation

This sub-clause provides that the Contract Price shall be adjusted to take account of an increase or decrease in Cost which arises from a change in the Laws of the Country (including new laws, modifications or repeated laws) arising after Base Date. Changes in Cost in other countries are not subject to the provisions of this sub-clause.

If the Contractor is delayed or incurs additional Cost, then, subject to the giving of notice in accordance with Sub-Clause 20.1, the Contractor is entitled to an extension of time and payment of Costs. Similarly, in accordance with the provisions of Sub-Clause 2.5, Employer's Claims, the Employer is entitled to a reduction of the Contract Price if there is a decrease in Costs.

The Contractor will be required to provide evidence of any increases in Cost (Government gazettes or other official notices).

This sub-clause will be equally applicable to the orders of local government bodies that may have appropriate legal powers to adjust prices.

It may happen that there may have been changes in Cost between Base Date and the issue of the Letter of Acceptance, particularly if the intervening period is unusually prolonged. Considering that neither Engineer nor Contractor will have been appointed or have a presence, it is submitted that the provisions of this sub-clause remain actionable and are to be dealt with as soon as practical after signature of the Contract.

13.8 Adjustment for Changes in Cost

In preparing a tender, a well-managed contractor will endeavour to manage the risks inherent in the execution of a contract to acceptable levels.

Consequently the provisions of this sub-clause are significant to the Contractor, as the risks from changes in Cost are reduced to more predictable and manageable levels.

This sub-clause provides a mechanism by the use of a formula designed to adjust the contract values to reflect changes in Cost during the period of escalation.

The Contractor will select which indices will be used and which will reflect his own accumulated experience and also his anticipated sources of the specified goods and services.

Not all potential changes in Cost are the subject of this formula and the Contractor may not agree with all the coefficients provided by the Employer and will need to make provisions elsewhere in his tender pricing.

In particular the formula includes a coefficient 'a' which represents the non-adjustable portion in contractual payments. There is a general consideration that the Contractor should be able to evaluate changes in Cost for the first year of a project with reasonable confidence and coefficient 'a' reflects that consideration.

In the course of the Contract the Contractor will be required to provide official data confirming the value of the indices, usually at monthly intervals. These can be obtained from national statistical offices or from the European Union statistical office.

Typically the values of these indices are issued 2–3 months after the period to which they refer. Consequently the preparation of Interim Payment Applications will require the use of provisional values which will require later adjustments to be made once final data become available.

The application of this sub-clause is varied should the Contractor fail to complete the Works within the Time for Completion, when *'adjustment of prices thereafter shall be made using either (i) each index or price applicable on the date 49 days prior to the expiry of the Time for Completion of the Works, or (ii) the current index or price: whichever is more favourable to the Employer'*.

Clause 14 Contract Price and Payment

14.1 The Contract Price

The Contract Price means the price defined in Sub-Clause 14.1 and all adjustments made in accordance with the Contract (Sub-Clause 12.3, Evaluation, refers). It is therefore a value which will increase in time.

The Contractor is required to pay all taxes. Exceptions have to be stated and these exceptions are likely to include VAT and customs duties.

14.2 Advance Payment

An Advance Payment is an interest-free loan provided to the Contractor by the Employer for mobilisation. It is appropriate that the Employer requests evidence that the Advance Payment has been spent for the intended purpose. As a pre-condition to payment of the Advance Payment, the Contractor shall provide the Employer with an Advance Payment guarantee. FIDIC provides a model form for this purpose. The guarantee should remain valid until the advance is repaid and not given a fixed expiry date. To avoid the possibility of forgeries being offered, the Employer may consider checking the validity of the guarantee directly with the provider.

14.3 Application for Interim Payment Certificates

This sub-clause requires that the Statement is submitted in six copies to the Engineer in a form approved by him.

The Statement shall include:

(a) the estimated value of Works performed to date
(b) the amounts to be added for changes in legislation
(c) the amount to be deducted for retention
(d) the amount to be added or deducted for Advance Payments and repayments
(e) the value of Plant and Materials on Site
(f) any other amounts due including claims (Clause 20)
(g) the deduction of previous amounts paid.

The preparation of the Statement can be time consuming and it is in the mutual interest of both Engineer and Contractor if the process of measurement and preparation of the Statement are coordinated. The larger and more complex the project, the greater is the effort required to prepare and agree the measurement to be used in the compilation of the Statement. The FIDIC Contracts Guide notes '*(there is) little point in calculating to an accuracy better than the contract value of the work executed per week*'. Items of work already completed or nearing completion can be measured in advance. The Engineer may be restricted in his ability to agree to on account payments and the Contractor is likely to leave items which cannot be readily resolved and measured for settlement in the next period rather than significantly delay the process of preparing the Interim Payment Statement.

14.4 Schedule of Payments

In substitution of the process of measurement described in Sub-Clause 14.3 above, payments under the Contract may be governed by a Schedule of Payments. There are a number of ways in which the Schedule of Payments may be drawn up. If this is not already provided for in the Contract Documents, then the Engineer and the Contractor will need to agree on the contents of a breakdown of the Schedule.

14.5 Plant and Materials intended for the Works

The Contractor is entitled to include in his Statement for the next Interim Payment Certificate an amount for Plant and Materials which have been delivered to the Site for inclusion in the permanent Works.

In support of any application, the Contractor shall provide the Engineer with satisfactory records, including proof of the cost of purchase and the cost of transport to site. The Engineer may also require evidence that the Plant and Materials are of the quality required by the Contract (although formal quality control procedures may follow later).

The Plant and Materials may be limited in scope to a listing provided in the Appendix to Tender, but more commonly it is left to the Contractor to identify the Plant and Materials he wishes to have included in the Interim Payment Certificate. Typically the Contractor's request will include Materials such as cement, structural steel, reinforcing steel, asphalt, and Plant will include mechanical and electrical machinery. The Contractor's request may also include Plant and Materials provided by subcontractors.

The Contractor is also entitled to include in his Statement the value of Plant and Materials which have been shipped but not yet delivered to Site. To support his application, the Contractor will be required to provide shipping documents as evidence of shipment together with insurance and a bank guarantee. Considering that major items of Plant may already be subject to stage payments, the Contractor may decide it is administratively more convenient to delay his application until the Plant has arrived on Site.

The Contractor may manufacture some Materials, notably aggregates, on Site and is likely to request payment under the provisions of this sub-clause, should the value of the Materials be significant. It would be necessary for the Engineer to assess a suitable unit rate for such items.

Throughout the execution of the Works the amount and value of Plant and Materials will rise and fall as fresh supplies arrive and items are consumed. As a consequence, the Engineer will have to measure or otherwise evaluate the amount and value of the Plant and Materials actually available on Site at the date of measurement. This value automatically reduces to zero once the Permanent Works are complete and the surplus, if any, reverts to the Contractor.

Plant and Materials are to be appropriately stored on Site at the Contractor's risk and expense.

The amount to be certified is stated to be 80% of the on-site cost of the Plant and Materials, but it is not uncommon for this percentage to be varied either in the Appendix to Tender or in the Particular Conditions of Contract. The currencies for the additional payment are to be those in which the payment will become due when the Plant and Materials are included in the Application for Interim Payment Certificates (refer to Sub-Clause 14.3(a)).

14.6 Issue of Interim Payment Certificates

It is not required to include the Advance Payment in an Interim Payment Certificate since such payment is subject to special payment conditions (see also Sub-Clause 14.7 following). It may be convenient for the Employer if the Engineer were to issue a unique payment certificate for the Advance Payment.

Until such time the Employer has received and approved the Performance Security provided by the Contractor, no amount will be certified or paid. *'Thereafter the Engineer shall within 28 days after he received a Statement and supporting documents from the Contractor, issue to the Employer (with a copy to the Contractor) an Interim Payment Certificate in which the Engineer fairly determines to be due with supporting particulars.'*

No Interim Payment Certificate will be issued with a value less than the minimum amount stated in the Appendix to Tender.

The Engineer is empowered to correct or modify any previous Interim Payment Certificate.

In theory the Contractor has the possibility to provide a Statement to the Engineer without any pre-discussion. The Engineer is left with the task of unilaterally deciding the actual amount due to the Contractor and will issue his Interim Payment Certificate accordingly.

However, in a majority of countries where FIDIC-based contracts are in use, it is common practice for the Engineer and Contractor to identify and negotiate the various elements to be included in any Interim Payment Certificate, leaving unresolved items for further negotiation and possible inclusion in another Interim Payment Application.

This is taken to extremes in some countries, where the accountancy rules of the Employer's Treasury Department may require the Contractor to sign the Interim Payment Certificate as a pre-condition to payment, even though he quite probably has a number of existing complaints and claims which remain unresolved. In such irregular situations a more knowledgeable Contractor may elect to provide a separate supplementary listing of all unpaid or unresolved items and include the same in the Progress Report described in Sub-Clause 4.21.

14.7 Payment

This sub-clause details the time intervals provided for the Employer to make payment to the Contractor.

(a) Advance Payment (see also introductory note Sub-Clause 14.6 above). The (first) instalment of the Advance payment shall be paid within 42 days after issuing the Letter of Acceptance or within 21 days of receiving the documents specified in Sub-Clause 4.2 (Performance Security) and Sub-Clause 14.2 (Advance Payment) whichever is earlier.

(b) Interim Payment Certificates. Sub-Clause 14.6 provides that the Engineer shall supply an Interim Payment Certificate to the Employer within 28 days of receiving a Statement from the Contractor. The Employer is allowed 56 days, measured from the date of receipt of the Contractor's Statement by the Engineer, in which to make payment to the Contractor. Any variation in the period required by the Engineer to make his certification has a corresponding effect on the time available to the Employer in which to make payment.

14.8 Delayed Payment

Should payments due to the Contractor be delayed past due date, he is entitled to be paid financing charges compounded monthly on the unpaid amount for the period of delay.

Financing charges are to be calculated at an annual rate of 3% above the discount rate of the Central Bank in the country of the currency of payment and paid in that currency.

Exceptionally the Contractor shall be entitled to this payment without formal notice under Sub-Clause 20.1 or certification by the Engineer.

The discount rates will be obtained from the Central Bank of the country for the local currency portion, and from a foreign central bank or organisation, e.g. European Union Statistics Office, for the foreign currency portion.

It is possible that the Contractor may be willing to accept payment entirely in local currency. This possibility has to be negotiated between the Employer and the Contractor.

14.9 Payment of Retention Money

The payment of Retention Money is divided into two phases:

(a) Issue of the Taking-Over Certificate. Once the Taking-Over Certificate has been issued, the Engineer shall proceed to certify for payment the first half of the Retention Money. However, if a Taking-Over Certificate is issued for a Section or part of the Works, then a 40% portion of the Retention Money for the Section or part of the Work is to be certified for payment. The amount to be released is defined as two-fifths of the proportion calculated by dividing the estimated contract value of the Section or part, by the estimated final Contract Price. Since the calculation is based on estimates which have no value elsewhere in the Contract, it is appropriate that the Engineer or Contractor co-operate to simplify the estimating process as far as possible.

(b) After expiry of the latest expiry dates of the Defects Notification Periods. Promptly after the latest expiry dates of the Defects Notification Periods, the outstanding balance of Retention Money shall be certified by the Engineer for payment. If a Taking-Over Certificate was issued for a Section or part of the Works, a further 40% portion of the Retention Money shall be certified for payment by the Engineer for payment.

The Engineer is entitled to withhold certification of the estimated value of any outstanding work until it is executed.

When calculating these proportions, no account shall be taken of any adjustments under Sub-Clause 13.7, Adjustments for Changes in Legislation, and Sub-Clause 13.8, Adjustments for Changes in Cost.

Reference may also be made to the indicative calculations given in Appendix F of this book.

14.10 Statement at Completion

'*Within 84 days after receiving the Taking-Over Certificate, the Contractor is required to submit to the Engineer six copies of a Statement at completion with supporting documents showing*:

- *the value of work done in accordance with the Contract up to the date stated in the Taking-Over Certificate*
- *any further sums which the Contractor considers due.*' (This will include the value of unresolved claims and other outstanding matters)
- '*estimates of other amounts which the Contractor considers will become due to him under the Contract.*' (This will include the value of work outstanding.)

The Statement is important because it defines the maximum amount of revenue which could be due to the Contractor and equally indicates to the Employer the likely maximum amount of his financial commitment.

14.11 Application for Final Payment Certificate

'*Within 56 days after receiving the Performance Certificate the Contractor shall submit a draft final statement with supporting documents showing in detail in a form approved by the Engineer*

(a) *the value of all work done in accordance with the Contract.*' This will include the value of measured works, the value of varied works performed, the value of accepted claims, and amounts due under Sub-Clauses 13.7 and 13.8.
(b) '*any further sums which the Contractor considers to be due to him under the Contract or otherwise.*'

It is probable that the majority of Contractor's claims and other matters will have been resolved at this time, leaving only a limited number of items yet to be settled. The details and valuations of these unresolved items can be included here.

It is required that the Engineer and Contractor will review the draft Statement with the intent to resolve all outstanding issues. If this process proves unsuccessful, then the Engineer shall provide the Employer with an Interim Payment Certificate inclusive of all agreed items. Only once the remaining outstanding issues are resolved under Sub-Clause 20.4, Obtaining Dispute Adjudication Board's Decision, or Sub-Clause 20.5, Amicable Settlement, shall the Contractor submit a Final Statement to the Employer. If either Party refers a dispute to Arbitration, then the Final Statement cannot be provided.

14.12 Discharge

When submitting the Final Statement, the Contractor is required to provide a written discharge confirming that the total amounts shown in the Final Settlement represents full and final settlement of all monies due to the Contractor. A sample form of discharge is provided in the FIDIC Contracts Guide on page 253.

14.13 Issue of Final Payment Certificate

Within 28 days after receiving the Final Statement complete with written discharge, the Engineer shall issue to the Employer the Final Payment Certificate which includes all that is finally due to the Contractor, with due allowance for any credits due to the Employer from the Contractor.

14.14 Cessation of Employer's Liability

The Employer is not liable to the Contractor for any matter or thing in connection with the Contract or its execution unless the Contractor has made provision in the Final Statement.

This requirement has the effect of constraining the Contractor from presenting additional claims at a late stage of the Contract.

14.15 Currencies of Payment

If the Accepted Contract Amount is expressed in local currency only, the proportions and amounts of the local and foreign currencies shall be stated in the Appendix to Tender.

Other payments shall be made in the currency of expenditure. If no exchange rates are given in the Contract, they shall be those prevailing at Base Date as determined by the Central Bank of the country.

Clause 15 Termination by the Employer

15.1 Notice to Correct

'If the Contractor fails to carry out any obligation under the Contract, the Engineer may by notice require the Contractor to make good the failure and remedy it within a specified reasonable time.'

The giving of notice by the Engineer under this sub-clause is an important matter, as it is generally perceived as a prelude to termination by the Employer. The Contractor is well advised to take remedial action without undue delay.

The FIDIC Contracts Guide provides important guidance to the Engineer in respect of this notice if the Employer intends to rely on the notice to terminate the Contract. The notice should refer to this sub-clause, describe the Contractor's failure and specify a reasonable time to remedy the failure. However, there is no obligation for the notice to be given under this sub-clause before the Employer terminates the Contract.

15.2 Termination by the Employer

Termination of the Contract by the Employer is evidently a major event that needs to be approached with caution. Whilst the Engineer has a key role to play in the management process leading to a notice of termination, the services of a legal advisor is recommended to review the correctness of the reasons for termination and to prepare the notice of termination. This sub-clause lists six categories of default by the Contractor entitling the Employer to give notice of termination. Four of these categories relate to inadequate performance by the Contractor. The Employer may, on giving the Contractor 14 days notice, terminate the Contract and enter the Site. The two remaining categories relate to insolvency or bribery and corruption entitling the Employer to immediately terminate the Contract.

If the Employer gives notice of termination and wishes to withdraw it, the Parties may agree that the notice is of no effect and that the Contract is not terminated.

The FIDIC Contracts Guide notes that in the period of notice of termination the Contractor is obliged to secure and make safe the Site. However, considering that the Contractor's employees are likely to immediately depart if payment of their salaries and wages are not assured, this period of notice is invaluable to both Employer and Engineer to enable them to organise and prepare an orderly departure of the Contractor from the Site.

The Contractor is required to hand over all Contractor's Documents and other design documents. The Engineer is best placed to manage this hand-over. Further, it will be necessary to secure all Plant and Materials, particularly those already the property of the Employer under the terms of the Contract. The Employer may wish to purchase other items from the Contractor and arrangements need to be put in hand.

After termination the Employer may complete the Works and/or arrange for other entities to do so and may use any Plant and Materials, Contractor's Documents and other design documents to do so. Upon notice by the Employer, the Contractor is entitled to remove Contractor's Equipment and Temporary Works '*at or near the Site*'. The Employer is not permitted to prevent the Contractor removing from Site the Contractor's Equipment and Temporary Works unless allowed to do so by the Laws of the Country.

Whilst not mentioned in the FIDIC Contracts Guide under this heading, it is appropriate that

(a) the Employer gives notice of claim to the provider of the Performance Security (Sub-Clause 4.2) that the Contract has been terminated and that the Employer registers a formal claim in accordance with the terms of the Performance Security and Sub-Clause 4.2(d) and

(b) the Employer gives notice of claim to the provider of the Advance Payment Guarantee under Sub-Clause 14.2 that the Contract has been terminated and the Employer registers a formal claim in accordance with the terms of the Advance Payment Guarantee and Sub-Clause 14.2 (ultimate paragraph).

15.3 Valuation at Date of Termination

The Engineer may expect to be very active in supporting the Employer dealing with the aftermath of termination. Many of these activities are not specifically identified in the Contract but arise because of the relationship between the Employer and Engineer and the Engineer's detailed knowledge of the Site and the Contractor's organisation. Confirmatory instructions may need to be given by the Employer, should this requirement exceed the obligations of the Engineer under the terms of his service contract.

In addition to those duties, this sub-clause confers on the Engineer the duty to '*agree or determine*' the value of the Works, Goods and Contractor's Documents, and any other sums due to the Contractor.

The Engineer is required by Sub-Clause 3.5, Determinations, to '*consult with each Party in an endeavour to reach an agreement…*'. Therefore it is appropriate to formally involve the Contractor in the preparation of the valuation, which should commence as soon as possible after termination. It may be that the Contractor no longer has Site representation or is unwilling to co-operate. Consequently the Engineer should proceed cautiously and ensure every opportunity is provided to the Contractor to participate in the preparation of the valuation. Formal invitations by letter or e-mail are appropriate. If the Contractor refuses to attend or otherwise co-operate with the Engineer, then the Engineer will need to proceed unilaterally with the valuation.

In addition to the valuation of measured works, the Engineer has to consider a number of other issues, including the valuation of Goods, Contractor's Documents and other design documents, which are to be handed into the ownership of the Employer. Other difficulties arise from consideration of payment due for time-related items such as insurances and bonds.

The continuing provision of services to the Employer and Engineer due under the Contract will require that alternative arrangements are made if disruptions to the efforts of the Engineer to fulfil his duties under the Contract are to be avoided.

The Engineer should proceed expeditiously with the preparation of the valuation and present a draft valuation to the Parties for comment and consultation.

If after consultation either of the Parties is unable to agree with any aspect of the valuation, the Engineer shall determine the matter. Thereafter the dissenting Party shall refer the unresolved matter to the dispute resolution procedures given in the Contract.

15.4 Payment after Termination

Further payments to the Contractor, if any, will continue to be withheld until such time as:

(a) the cost of executing and completing any defects, damages for delay and similar costs have been established and
(b) the loss, damage or additional cost of completing the Works (either by the Employer or a replacement contractor) are known. This may not be possible until the Works are finally completed.

Once all these matters are finalised, any balance in favour of the Contractor will be due for payment to him. If there is any balance in favour of the Employer, then the amount due shall be paid by the Contractor to the Employer, failing which, the Employer shall be entitled to request payment from the provider of the Performance Security.

The repayment of any outstanding amount of the Advance Payment shall be requested by the Employer from the provider of the Advance Payment Guarantee immediately following notice of termination.

15.5 Employer's Entitlement to Termination

This sub-clause entitles the Employer to terminate the Contract at any time for the Employer's convenience. The termination shall take effect 28 days after the Employer gives notice or the Employer returns the Performance Security, whichever is the later.

The Employer is not permitted to terminate the Contract for the purpose of executing the Works himself or arranging for another contractor to execute the Works himself.

After termination, the Contractor shall proceed in accordance with Sub-Clause 16.3, Cessation of Work and Removal of Contractor's Equipment, and shall be paid in accordance with Sub-Clause 19.6, Optional Termination, Payment and Release.

The FIDIC Contracts Guide further comments that any payment to the Contractor has to be consistent with the applicable law and with the requirements of a public authority, Employer or international financial institution or other employer, as may be applicable.

It is emphasised that termination under the provisions of this sub-clause would be a rare event and subject to legal review before implementation.

Clause 16 Suspension and Termination by the Contractor

16.1 Contractor's Entitlement to Suspend Work

The Contractor is entitled to suspend the Works under the following circumstances:

(a) the Engineer fails to certify in accordance with Sub-Clause 14.6, Issue of Interim Payment Certificates or
(b) the Employer fails to comply with Sub-Clause 2.4, Employer's Financial Arrangements or
(c) the Employer fails to make payment when due.

The Contractor shall give not less than 21 days notice to the Employer (not the Engineer) of his intent to suspend work (or reduce rate of work) unless and until the Contractor has received the Payment Certificate or evidence of payment. Notice cannot be given in advance and can only be given in the event of actual failure.

The Contractor shall restart work as soon as possible after resolution of the cause of delayed payment.

Payments to the Contractor may be made only in part and not in full and as a consequence the Contractor may not be able to finance all programmed operations. In such circumstances it would be appropriate for the Engineer and Contractor to establish which areas of work shall be given priority.

The Contractor's entitlement to payment of financing charges, Sub-Clause 14.8, Delayed Payments, and to terminate the Contract, Sub-Clause 16.2, Termination by Contractor, are not affected by the Contractor suspending the Works.

Subject to compliance with Sub-Clause 20.1, the Contractor is entitled to claim an extension of time, Sub-Clause 8.4, and Payment of Cost and Profit.

16.2 Termination by Contractor

The Contract provides eight conditions which entitle the Contractor to terminate the Contract. Terminations by the Contractor are frequently linked to financial disputes, particularly those related to any failure of the Employer to pay amounts to the Contractor when due. The Engineer is involved only if the Engineer fails to issue the relevant Payment Certificate within 56 days of receipt of a Statement from the Contractor. The Contractor is required to give 14 days' notice of termination to the Employer.

The Parties may subsequently jointly agree that the notice of termination is of no effect and that the Contract is not terminated.

16.3 Cessation of Work and Removal of Contractor's Equipment

After notice of termination under Sub-Clause 15.5, Employer's Entitlement to Termination, Sub-Clause 16.2, Termination by Contractor, or Sub-Clause

19.6, Optional Termination, Payment and Release, has taken effect, the Contractor shall promptly:

(a) cease all further work
(b) hand over Contractor's Documents, Materials and other work for which the Contractor has been paid
(c) remove all other Goods from the Site and leave the Site.

Inevitably the Engineer will be involved in assisting the Employer in the management of this process of closing the Site.

16.4 Payment on Termination

After notice of termination under Sub-Clause 16.2, Termination by Contractor, has taken effect, the Employer shall promptly:

- return the Performance Security to the Contractor
- pay the Contractor in accordance with Sub-Clause 19.6, Optional Termination, Payment and Release, and
- pay to the Contractor any loss or profit or other loss or damage.

It is to be noted that Sub-Clause 14.2 requires the Contractor to repay the outstanding amount of the Advance Payment immediately on termination.

Again the Engineer will need to be involved in assisting the Employer to manage the requirements of this sub-clause.

Clause 17 Risk and Responsibility

17.0 General

The Engineer has no input into the allocation of risk and responsibilities between the Parties. The allocation is as stated in the Contract. However, it is likely that the Engineer may be called upon to make decisions in respect of events which arise during the execution of the Works.

17.1 Indemnities

In this sub-clause the risks and responsibilities inherent in the Contract are identified and allocated between the Parties.

With due regard to their allocated share of the total risk, each Party shall indemnify the other Party from claims including those from third parties, arising out of the Contractor's execution of the Works.

This sub-clause describes the allocation of the risk in precise terms and can be summarised as follows:

(a) The Contractor is required to indemnify the Employer, the Employer's Personnel and their agents in respect of:
- bodily injury, sickness, disease or death of any person arising from the execution of the Works unless attributable to negligence or wilful act of the Employer
- damage to or loss of property arising out of the execution of the Works
- damage or loss attributable to any negligence or breach of the Contract by the Contractor

(b) the Employer is required to indemnify the Contractor, the Contractor's Personnel and their agents in respect of all claims relating to:
- bodily injury, sickness, disease or death which is attributable to the Employer, the Employer's Personnel and their agents
- matters for which liability may be excluded from insurance cover in Sub-Clause 18.3, sub-paragraph (d).

17.2 Contractor's Care of Works

'The Contractor has full responsibility for the care of the Works and Goods from the Commencement Date until the Taking-Over Certificate is issued, ...when responsibility passes to the Employer.

If loss or damage occurs to the Works, Goods or Contractor's Documents during the period when the Contractor is responsible for their care, for any cause not listed in Sub-Clause 17.3, Employer's Risks, the Contractor shall rectify the loss or damage at the Contractor's risk and cost.'

17.3 Employer's Risks

This sub-clause lists eight categories of events which are defined as Employer's Risks. The FIDIC Contracts Guide notes also that some of the Employer's Risks may also constitute Force Majeure events under Clause 19. Of these, five categories (a) – (e) list matters which typically refer to disturbances including war, rebellion, riot, munitions and pressure waves caused by supersonic waves.

Sub-Clause 17.3 (f) refers to *'use or occupation by the Employer of any part of the Permanent Works, except as may be specified in the Contract'*. The formal taking over process is governed by Sub-Clauses 10.1 and 10.2. Sub-Clause 10.2(a) which specifically states that *'if the Employer does use any part of the Works before the Taking-Over Certificate is issued, the part which is used shall be deemed to have been taken over as from the date on which it is used'*.

As a consequence, if the Employer requires occupation of a part of the Works for a limited period, it would be appropriate for him to negotiate a separate agreement with the Contractor. Care should be taken not to invalidate the Contract insurances.

As reported in commentary on Sub-Clauses 10.1 and 10.2, taking over in this manner may not conform to the local law.

Sub-Clause 17.1(g) defines as an Employer's risk the *'design of any part of the Works by the Employer's personnel or by others for whom the Employer is responsible…'*. Difficulties of interpretation may arise if the causes of a failure are not readily apparent or if the failure arose from a number (or combination) of events.

Sub-Clause 17.1(h) defines as an Employer's risk *'the operation of the forces of nature which is Unforeseeable or which an experienced contractor could not reasonably have been expected to have taken adequate preventative precautions'*. In contrast it will be noted that Sub-Clause 4.12, Unforeseeable Physical Conditions, specifically excludes climatic conditions.

The term 'Unforeseeable' is defined in Sub-Clause 1.1.6.8 as meaning *'not reasonably foreseeable by an experienced contractor by the date for Submission of the Tender'*. The FIDIC Contracts Guide offers an opinion that an event which occurred once every six years might be foreseeable, but an event which took place once every 10 years might be considered 'unforeseeable'.

The Contractor could be reasonably expected to support a claim by reference to official data and reports.

The FIDIC Contracts Guide warns that the Employer may not be wholly responsible for all the consequences listed in this Sub-Clause 17.3. Sub-Clause 17.4 only entitles the Contractor to compensation for rectifying loss or damage attributable to the Employer's Risks. Consequently, other losses, not otherwise an Employer's Risk, will not fall under the scope of Sub-Clause 17.4.

17.4 Consequences of Employer's Risks

Should there occur an event which is an Employer's Risk, then the Contractor, having given notice in accordance with Sub-Clause 20.1, Contractor's Claims, shall be entitled to an extension of time and payment of cost incurred.

For events identified under Sub-Clauses 17.3(f) and 17.3(g), the Contractor shall also be entitled to reasonable profit.

The FIDIC Contracts Guide further comments that this provision only entitles the Contractor to '*compensation for rectifying loss and damage but does not limit his entitlement under Sub-Clause 19.4, Consequences of Force Majeure*'.

17.5 Intellectual and Industrial Property Rights

The Employer shall indemnify the Contractor against any claim which arises as an unavoidable result of the Contractor's compliance with the Contract or the result of any Works used by the Employer for a purpose other than inferred from the Contract or in conjunction with anything supplied by the Contractor, unless the use was disclosed to the Contractor prior to the Base Date or is stated in the Contract.

The Contractor shall indemnify the Employer against any claim which arises out of the manufacture, use, sale or import of any Goods or any design for which the Contractor is responsible.

A Party is required to give notice of claim to the other Party within 28 days of having received a claim alleging infringement from a third party.

This topic can be complex and legal advice should be obtained.

17.6 Limitation of Liability

'*Neither Party shall be liable to the other Party for the loss of use of any Works, loss of profit or any direct or consequential loss or damage which may be suffered by the other Party in connection with the Contract.*' (Exceptions noted.)

With minor exceptions '*the total liability of the Contractor or the Employer… shall not exceed the sum stated in the Particular Conditions or if not so stated, the Accepted Contract Amount*'.

In some jurisdictions the Contractor may be required to provide decennial liability for hidden defects for 10 years from completion.

Clause 18 Insurance

18.0 General

A key purpose of insurance is to ensure that in the event of a significant loss or damage the Contractor will retain sufficient financial capacity to complete the Works. At the same time the Contractor will wish to ensure that his own financial stability is not threatened. The Employer may decide to insure to enable him to finance rectification works which arise from an Employer's risk event. This is particularly likely for a privately financed Employer. However, many employers who are state-owned may have internal rules and regulations which permit the Employer to be self-insured.

The general terms of the required insurances will have been set out by the Employer in the Contract Data (notably in the Appendix to Tender) and consequently the role of the Engineer will be to ensure that the Contractor is in compliance with the requirements of the Contract.

Prior to tender the Employer will have decided which Party will be the insuring Party and who will become responsible for arranging the insurances specified in the Contract. Particularly if more than one Contract is to be executed on the Site in approximately the same time period, the Employer may decide it is commercially advantageous for him to become the insuring Party with a global insurance covering all contracts on the Site. For single contracts it is more likely that the Contractor will be nominated as the insuring Party.

18.1 General Requirements for Insurances

If the Contractor is the insuring Party, the insurances shall be obtained from approved insurers and on terms approved by the Employer. These terms are to be agreed prior to issue of the Letter of Acceptance and shall take precedence over the provisions of this Clause.

Contractors who routinely work in the field of international construction are very likely to use insurers with whom they have a long-term relationship and who are likely to offer better terms.

When the Employer is the insuring Party, each insurance shall be consistent with the details attached to the Particular Conditions (Appendix to Tender). The Contractor will need to be informed of the terms of the insurances and is likely to request information on the amount of deductibles.

Each Party is required to comply with the terms of the Insurances. No changes are to be made to the insurances unless agreed by both Parties.

The terms of the Contract may require that the Parties are to be jointly insured, but arranged as if each Party were insured separately. It needs to be established if the Insurers will pay claims directly to the Party making the claim, or whether payments will be initially directed to a joint account for eventual distribution as agreed by the Parties.

Contractors may include subcontractors in these insurances, but the Contractor will remain responsible for any consequences. Subcontractors will not be paid directly by the insurers.

Payments made from insurers shall be used to rectify loss or damage and shall be made in the currencies of the Contract.

The FIDIC Contracts Guide provides a warning that not all risks may be insured.

18.2 Insurance for Works and Contractor's Equipment

This sub-clause describes a requirement for two differing scopes of insurance.

Unless stated otherwise in the Particular Conditions, both types of insurance are to be provided by the Contractor as the insuring party and shall be in the joint names of the Parties, who shall be jointly entitled to receive payments from the insurers. As a consequence, it will be necessary for the Parties to establish a joint bank account from which payments are to be made to either Party for the purpose of rectifying loss or damage.

(a) Insurance for Works (familiarly referred to as 'Contractor's All Risk')

Sub-Clause 17.2, Care of the Works, requires that the Contractor takes full responsibility for the care of the Works and Goods. The scope of the insurance shall cover full reinstatement costs including the cost of demolition and clearing of the Site, together with any engineering cost or other professional fees.

The insurance shall be valid and submitted to the Employer within the period specified in the Appendix to Tender calculated from Commencement Date and shall remain valid to provide cover until the issue of a Taking-Over Certificate, when responsibility passes to the Employer. The insurance shall continue to provide cover for any ongoing operations, particularly those relating to outstanding works and defects liability obligations and shall terminate on the date of issue of the Performance Certificate.

Excluded from the scope of this insurance is any loss or damage in respect of:

(a) a part of the Works that is defective due to a design fault
(b) a part of the Works that itself becomes lost or damaged in order to reinstate another part that is lost or in a defective condition
(c) Works taken over by the Employer.

The Contractor may be unwilling to disclose the amount of the insurance premium. However, it is likely that the insurers will vary the premium should the final Contract Price exceed the Contract Price or if the Time for Completion is exceeded.

(b) Contractor's Equipment

Many contractors will have a long-term relationship with their insurers and are likely to obtain insurance for Contractor's Equipment on favourable terms. Some of the larger contractors are likely to have a 'pool' of equipment available for all their projects which is continuously insured, ready for allocation to their project sites. The Engineer should be aware that insurance premiums paid by a Contractor may be difficult to establish with complete accuracy. Consequently, should a Contractor have a valid claim for Extension of Time and payment for extended costs, it may be difficult to evaluate extended insurance costs not least because the insurer may take the opportunity to inflate the cost of premiums for any extension.

Although the Contractor is required to replace damaged or written-off Contractor's Equipment, the reality is that the Contractor may no longer have a physical need to replace the Contractor's Equipment and/or the replacement will arrive on site too late to be of use.

In the event of a loss or damage, the Contractor's claim will be evaluated by a loss adjudicator ('loss assessor') acting on behalf of the insurers. The claim will be assessed on the basis of direct cost (proven by the Contractor) plus a nominal overhead percentage (10% is typical) and thus is unlikely to match the Contractor's actual total loss.

18.3 Insurance against Injury to Persons and Damage to Property, Familiarly Referred to as 'Third Party Insurance'

The Contractor (defined as the insuring Party) shall insure against each Party's liability for any loss, damage, bodily injury which may occur to any physical property (except things insured under Sub-Clause 18.2) or to any person (except persons insured under Sub-Clause 18.4) which may arise out of the Contractor's performance of the Contract and occurring before the issue of the Performance Certificate.

The insurance shall be for a fixed limit per occurrence as stated in the Appendix to Tender, with no limit on the number of occurrences. This sub-clause continues *'if an amount is not stated in the Appendix to Tender, this sub-clause shall not apply'*. It is understood that it is the whole of the sub-clause which *'shall not apply'* and not some part. An omission would potentially expose both Parties to potentially significant claims and the Parties should reconsider the matter and take out supplementary insurance as appropriate.

18.4 Insurance for Contractor's Personnel

The Contractor is required to provide insurance against liability for claims and damages arising from injury, sickness, disease or death of any person employed by the Contractor or any other Contractor's Personnel. Contractor's Personnel includes the Contractor's subcontractors. For administrative convenience, the Contractor would prefer his subcontractors to provide insurance for their own employees. The Contractor remains responsible for compliance with this sub-clause by the subcontractor's personnel. Care is to be taken that subcontractors and suppliers visiting the Site are also covered.

The provision of this type of insurance may be required by law. As an employment inducement the Contractor may find it appropriate to supplement any state insurance scheme.

Foreign workers employed as expatriates may also be covered by law, which is likely to be supplemented in their individual employment contracts.

The Engineer may find it appropriate from time to time to request the Contractor to provide evidence of compliance with the requirements of this sub-clause.

Clause 19 Force Majeure

19.1 Definition of Force Majeure

Force Majeure is defined as an '*exceptional event or circumstance*' and '*the event must be exceptional and not merely usual*'.

The Contract identifies four criteria which need to be satisfied if an occurrence is to constitute a Force Majeure event:

- it is to be beyond a Party's control
- the affected Party could not reasonably have made provision for it
- the affected Party could not have avoided or overcome it
- it must not be substantially attributable to the other Party, in which case it will be subject to other contractual provisions.

Force Majeure may include but not be limited to man-made events including war, rebellion, riots, munitions (as also described in Sub-Clause 17.3, Employer's Risks).

In addition, Sub-Clause 19.1(v) also defines natural catastrophes such as earthquake, hurricane, typhoon and volcanic activity as Force Majeure events. This contrasts with the provision of Sub-Clause 17.3(v), Employer's Risks, for '*any operation of the forces of nature which is unforeseeable or against which an experienced contractor could not reasonably have been expected to have taken adequate preventative precautions*'.

The differentiation between these differing provisions is assumed to reflect the degree of severity of the event. Under the provisions of Clause 17, there is an underlying presumption that the Works will continue, whereas Clause 19 provides for the possibility of termination and release from performance.

The FIDIC Contracts Guide notes '*Sub-Clause 19.4 does not limit the Contractor's entitlements under Sub-Clause 17.4*'.

19.2 Notice of Force Majeure

In the event of Force Majeure the affected Party is required to notify the other Party within 14 days of the event or occurrence. The notice should not only identify the Force Majeure event, but also how it will prevent the execution of the Works.

The examples are given of typical events and circumstances listed in this sub-clause. These Force Majeure events are in some parts identical to the Employer's Risks listed in Sub-Clause 17.3. However, there is likely to be some variation in interpretation consequent upon the pre-conditions listed in Sub-Clause 17.3.

19.3 Duty to Minimise Delay

Each Party shall make every effort to minimise any delay arising as a consequence of Force Majeure.

19.4 Consequences of Force Majeure

Should a Force Majeure event occur, the Contractor having given notice under Sub-Clause 19.2 and having complied with Sub-Clause 20.1, shall be entitled to:

- an extension of time in accordance with Sub-Clause 8.4
- reimbursement of Cost arising from man-made events (war, rebellion, riot, munitions), but not from natural catastrophes occurring in the Country.

19.5 Force Majeure Affecting Subcontractor

If the terms of a subcontract gives the subcontractor greater relief than the subcontractor is entitled to under Clause 19, then the Contractor is not entitled to the same enhanced relief under the Contract.

19.6 Optional Termination, Payment and Release

This sub-clause provides for the event that it may not be possible to continue with the Works, at least for the foreseeable future, as a consequence of a Force Majeure event.

Should the execution of the Works be substantially prevented for a continuous period of 84 days or for multiple periods totalling 140 days as a consequence of Force Majeure, then either Party may give notice of termination to take effect 7 days after notice is given. In catastrophic situations the Parties may decide the notice shall have immediate effect.

Thereafter the Engineer shall proceed to finalise the Contract in a manner similar to that described in Sub-Clause 15.3, Valuation at Date of Termination.

19.7 Release from Performance under Law

In extreme examples of Force Majeure it may be impossible or unlawful for either or both Parties to fulfil their contractual obligations. Either Party may give notice to the other Party of the circumstances of the Force Majeure. Thereafter the Parties are discharged from further performance. Any sum to be paid by the Employer to the Contractor shall be determined by the Engineer as if the Contract had been terminated under Sub-Clause 19.6 above.

Clause 20 Claims, Disputes and Arbitration

20.0 General

This sub-clause describes in detail the procedures to be followed by the Parties to resolve claims and disputes, including referral to international arbitration if necessary.

There are a number of permutations made possible by the content of this Clause. It is a requirement that the Employer will have precisely stated his requirements in the Particular Conditions.

Sub-Clause 3.5, Determinations, requires that the Engineer will agree or determine any matter. Having given his determination, the Engineer has fulfilled his quasi judicial role. The Parties may agree with or dispute the Engineer's Decision. Either Party may then refer any dispute to the Dispute Adjudication Board in the manner given in this Clause. The Engineer has the right to become the agent of the Employer and may represent the Employer in any future proceedings.

20.1 Contractor's Claims

This sub-clause describes, step by step, the procedures to be followed by the Contractor if he considers himself entitled to an extension of time, additional payment or both.

(i) The Contractor is obliged to give notice to the Engineer of the event or circumstance giving rise to the claim. The notice shall be given as soon as practical, but not later than 28 days after becoming aware of the event or circumstance.

(ii) The notice shall describe the event or circumstance and should identify the clause of the Contract which the Contractor considers entitles him to claim. The notice may refer to more than one clause. The notice need not be fully detailed but should identify the claim in sufficient detail.

(iii) The notice of claim shall be sent to the Engineer with a copy to the Employer as required. No response is required from the Engineer except to acknowledge receipt.

(iv) If the Contractor fails to give notice within 28 days, the Contractor will lose all his entitlement. The sub-clause states emphatically *'the Contractor shall not be entitled…'*. The Engineer has no power to vary this condition regardless of protestations from the Contractor. (NB, One possible exception arises if there is an event or circumstance which arises in the interval between presentation of tenders and award of contract which is not known to the Parties. A typical example could be a state-controlled change in the price of fuels. It is considered that this type of event would have to be resolved directly between the Employer and Contractor.).

(v) The Contractor shall keep detailed records which should be copied to the Engineer or made available for inspection. The Contractor may be reluctant to provide copies of confidential records, including those of his personnel, but is more likely to allow inspection and provide extracts. Wherever possible, it is beneficial if the Engineer agrees with the Contractor records of site activities *'for record purposes only'*. Good record keeping is essential.

(vi) Within 42 days after becoming aware of the event or circumstance giving rise to the claim, the Contractor shall submit to the Engineer a fully detailed claim. If the claim is complex and requiring extensive research, the Contractor may request an extension of the period for submittal which has to be approved by the Engineer.

(vii) If the event or circumstance giving rise to the claim has a continuing effect, the fully detailed claim described in (vi) above shall be considered an interim claim. The Contractor shall provide further interim claims at monthly intervals. A final claim shall be sent within 28 days after the end of the effects of the event or circumstance. Typically this would apply to claims caused by events described in Sub-Clause 13.7, Adjustment for Changes in Legislation, and Sub-Clause 13.8, Adjustment for Changes in Cost.

(viii) Within 42 days after receiving the Contractor's claim (or any other period proposed by the Engineer and agreed by the Contractor), the Engineer shall respond with approval or disapproval and detailed comments. He may request further particulars but shall give his response on the principles of the claim within such time.

(ix) The Engineer shall include in each following Payment Certificate amounts which are reasonably substantiated. Frequently the Particular Conditions include a provision preventing the Engineer from approving additional payments to the Contractor, unless approved by the Employer. This provision implies that the Employer and the Engineer will have received the conclusions (and recommendations) of the Engineer in good time, in order that payments due to the Contractor are not unduly delayed, and resulting in further claims from the Contractor.

(x) The Engineer shall proceed in accordance with the procedures stated in Sub-Clause 3.5, Determinations, to agree or determine the extension of time and additional payment due to the Contractor. Thereafter, if either Party is dissatisfied with the determination of the Engineer, they are entitled to refer the matter to the Dispute Adjudication Board (DAB).

20.2 Appointment of a Dispute Adjudication Board

The FIDIC Contracts Guide describes three types of Dispute Adjudication Board (DAB):

- a full-term DAB with one member. If a list of potential members is provided in the Contract, the Parties shall agree the single member
- a full-term DAB with three members. Each Party shall nominate one member for approval by the other Party. The Parties shall consult with

both members and agree upon a third member who shall be appointed as Chairman. It is considered beneficial if the Chairman has some legal experience. The FIDIC Contracts Guide considers that a three member full-term DAB is appropriate for a contract with a monthly valuation exceeding €2.0 million and where the work is sufficiently complex, requiring many variations
- an 'ad hoc' DAB with one or three members appointed if and when a particular dispute arises. This is considered most appropriate if the design and manufacture of a Plant is a substantial part of the contract.

DAB members should be appropriately qualified and have experience in the type of construction required by the Contract. They must be impartial and to avoid doubt should not have previously been in the employ of either Party or associated organisations. In addition to proficiency in the language of the Contract it is recommended that they be of different nationality to either of the Parties.

It is the intention that the DAB shall be appointed and functional before the Contractor starts work. For a variety of reasons, this early mobilisation is rarely achieved, which is unfortunate since a disproportionate number of disputes do arise in the early stages of construction. Every effort should be made to minimise delays in bringing the DAB to operational status.

20.3   Failure to Agree Dispute Adjudication Board

This sub-clause provides the conditions and procedures to be followed in the event of the Parties failing to nominate a member for approval or otherwise prevent the formation of a DAB.

Should the Parties be unable to agree on the appointment of a sole member, a nomination for a member or the chairman of a three member DAB or a replacement member, then the appointing entity or official named in the Appendix to Tender shall, on the request of either or both Parties, consult with both Parties in appointing a member.

20.4   Obtaining Dispute Adjudication Board's Decision

A full-term DAB will typically visit the site every 3--4 months. During periods between visits they require that they be kept aware of progress and events of significance. Standard practice is that the Employer, assisted by the Engineer, provides information packages to the Chairman of the DAB who then redistributes the information to the other members of the DAB. The Contractor is both expected and entitled to make his contribution to this flow of information to the DAB. During their visit to site, it is likely that the DAB will ask the Parties to inform them of any disputes (actual or potential) or other matters which could affect the progress of the Works.

This is the opportunity for the Parties, if they so wish, to refer a dispute or other matter to the DAB for their opinion (and not for a formal decision). This has the advantage that the opinion may help to resolve a dispute by exploring the alternatives available to the Parties. It is not necessary to prepare detailed papers, as matters can be conducted orally, but the preparation of a documents package will improve the understanding of the DAB. Typically, because the hearing is conducted orally, the DAB will expect to hear the opinions of the staff who are involved in the dispute and will not permit the involvement of lawyers and other external experts.

The DAB may prefer to comment either orally or in writing. The primary intention is to guide the Parties into avenues of approach which conceivably could help resolve or minimise a dispute with undue formality.

Collectively and individually the Parties can then assess the opinion offered by the DAB before making a formal request to the DAB for a decision under the provisions of Sub-Clause 20.4. The Engineer has a key role to play in obtaining the opinion of the DAB. He will be acting for the Employer and will be expected to provide detailed information on behalf of the Employer.

Should the informal approach to the DAB prove unsuccessful, either Party has the option to refer the dispute to the DAB for a formal decision. No matter can be formally referred to the DAB unless there is a dispute. The claims of the Employer and the Contractor are typically notified under Sub-Clauses 2.5 and 20.1 respectively and are subject to ongoing discussions and submissions followed by consultations. If the dispute is not resolved, then the Engineer shall make his decision under the provisions of Sub-Clause 3.5.

The FIDIC Contracts Guide offers that a dispute exists when

- a Party rejects the Engineer's determination
- discussions between the Parties have continued for a lengthy period without resolution
- one Party fails or declines to discuss the dispute with the other Party
- there is a minimal progress in finding a solution.

In considering any request for a decision, the DAB will first decide whether a dispute exists, using whatever criteria they consider appropriate.

In requesting a formal decision from the DAB, the claimant Party is required to provide a written reference, detailing the principles of the dispute, including details of the position of the claimant. This document is to be copied to both the other Party and the Engineer. The reference date is the date the document is received by the Chairman of the DAB. The defendant Party shall then provide documents detailing their counter-position.

The Employer and the Engineer should jointly review how this process will be managed. The Engineer's staff, who may be fully engaged on other activities, may require reinforcement to manage the additional work load resulting from this dispute procedure.

Having studied the presentation of both Parties, the DAB may require a formal meeting attended by the Parties to clarify any issues.

Within 84 days after receiving the original reference, the DAB will give its written decision, which is binding on both Parties and which shall be given with immediate effect. If either Party is dissatisfied with the decision of the DAB, notice shall be given to the other Party by giving notice of dissatisfaction within a period of 28 days after receiving the decision and thereafter is entitled to commence arbitration proceedings.

20.5 Amicable Settlement

Once notice of dissatisfaction has been given, both Parties shall make one more effort to settle matters amicably before commencing arbitration.

However, arbitration may be commenced on or before the 65th day after the date on which notice of dissatisfaction was given, even if no attempt at amicable settlement had been made.

20.6 Arbitration

Unless there is an amicable settlement, the dispute shall be finally settled under the Rules of Arbitration of the International Chambers of Commerce (the Particular Conditions will likely provide the rules of any arbitration together with the place of arbitration, the applicable law and the language of the arbitration).

The dispute is stated to be settled by three arbitrators, although the Parties may be agreeable to the use of a single arbitrator.

The arbitrators have full power to review every aspect of the dispute as they may decide, including any decision of the DAB.

Nothing shall prevent the Engineer from being called as a witness.

Arbitration may be commenced prior to or after completion of the Works.

20.7 Failure to Comply with Dispute Adjudication Board's Decision

Once a decision of the DAB has become binding and final, the Parties are obliged to give effect to it.

In the event that neither Party has given notice of dissatisfaction within the period stated in Sub-Clause 20.4, the related decision of the DAB, if any, has become final and binding, then should a Party fail to comply with this decision, the other Party may refer the failure itself to arbitration under Sub-Clause 20.6.

20.8 Expiry of Dispute Adjudication Board's Appointment

If a dispute arises and there is no DAB in place

- because of a Party's intransigence or
- the DABs appointment has expired upon the issue of the discharge described in Sub-Clause 14.2, Discharge,

then the dispute may be referred directly to arbitration under Sub-Clause 20.6, Arbitration.

Appendices

Appendix A
Conditions of Contract for Plant and Design-Build (1999) (P & DB) 'The Yellow Book'

The P & DB Conditions of Contract are intended for use where the Contractor designs and provides, in accordance with the Employer's requirements, fully functional plant and other works which may include architectural, civil, mechanical, electrical or other works.

The Employer's requirements, which are to be provided with the Invitation to Tender, have to be precisely defined if future claims concerning the scope and quality of the Works are to be avoided.

Not only is the Contractor responsible for design of the Works, but he also carries primary responsibility for the commissioning of the Works (including training of the Employer's or end-user's operational staff). In addition he will also be required to provide extensive documentation including as-built documents and operation manuals.

The Red Book, CONS form of contract requires that the Works are to be valued by a process of admeasurement based on a Bill of Quantities. In contrast, P & DB contracts are based on a lump sum (The Accepted Contract Amount), which for evaluation purposes is to be broken down into convenient smaller lump sums.

Occasionally hybrid P & DB contracts are encountered, which provide for some of the Works to be evaluated by reference to a Bill of Quantities and other parts to be valued as lump sums. The Employer risks the possibility that the Contractor's designer may not be overly concerned at the possibility of quantity overruns.

Those clauses of the P & DB contract that are amended from CONS, primarily as a consequence of the Contractor's design and commissioning responsibilities, are commented upon below.

Sub-Clause 1.5 – Priority of Documents

The Employer's Requirements are given a lower priority than both the General and Particular Conditions of Contract, but have a higher priority than the Contractor's Proposal provided with his tender.

An Employer's and Engineer's Guide to the FIDIC Conditions of Contract, First Edition. Michael D. Robinson.
© 2013 John Wiley & Sons, Ltd. Published 2013 by John Wiley & Sons, Ltd.

Sub-Clause 1.9 – Errors in Employer's Requirements

The consequences of any oversight made by the Contractor in the preparation of the Contractor's Proposal are to the account of the Contractor. The Contractor is required to demonstrate that there was an error in the Employer's Requirements if he intends to notify a claim under this sub-clause.

A review of tender correspondence (including 'Questions and Answers' exchanges) is likely to be a factor in adjudicating the validity of any Contractor's claim. Evidently the Engineer's responses to tender queries are to be clearly and comprehensively expressed.

Sub-Clause 4.6 – Co-operation

The Contractor is required to coordinate the activities of other contractors and to the extent specified in the Employer's Requirements.

If there are important consequences, these should be evaluated in the preparation of the Programme.

Sub-Clause 5.5 – Training

Sub-Clause 5.6 – As-Built Drawings

Sub-Clause 5.7 – Operation and Maintenance Manuals

These three activities are closely interconnected and their preparation and execution can be time-consuming. Adequate time for these activities must be allowed in the preparation of the Programme. Both the Employer (Sub-Clause 5.5 'Training') and the Engineer (Sub-Clause 5.6 'As-Built Drawings' and Sub-Clause 5.7 'Operation and Maintenance Manuals') will be involved in the timely completion of these tasks.

Sub-Clause 9.1 – Contractor's Obligations

The following Tests on Completion are specified:

- pre-commissioning tests (dry tests)
- commissioning tests (operational tests)
- trial operation (group or full load tests).

The Contractor is required to give 21 days notice of the intended date of executing these tests. There is a linkage to Sub-Clauses 5.5, 5.6 and 5.7. In particular it is important that the Employer's staff are involved in the performance of these tests as part of their training programme.

Sub-Clause 11.2 – Remedying Defects

This sub-clause makes the Contractor responsible for not only the consequences of faulty design or sub-standard Plant, Material or workmanship, but also for *'any improper operation or maintenance which was attributable to matters for which the Contractor is responsible (under Sub-Clauses 5.5 to 5.7 or otherwise)…'*.

Consequently the Contractor is responsible for any faulty operation or maintenance by the Employer if a failure arises as a consequence of any failure of the Contractor to fulfil the requirements of Sub-Clauses 5.5 – 5.7.

Sub-Clause 12.0 – Tests on Completion

Reference may be made to the summary quoted in Sub-Clause 9.1 above. This sub-clause deals with the execution of the Tests on Completion and with the remedies available to a Party in the event of a failure of the other Party to comply.

Sub-Clause 13.1 – Right to Vary

The detailed definition of a Variation given in CONS is replaced with a simple statement that either the Engineer or the Contractor can initiate a Variation. Further explanation can be found in the FIDIC Contracts Guide.

Sub-Clause 14.1 – The Contract Price

The Contract Price shall be the lump sum Accepted Contract Amount and is subject to adjustments in accordance with the Contract. The Works, once completed, are not required to be re-measured or re-evaluated.

Appendix B
Conditions of Contract for EPC/Turnkey Projects (EPCT) 'The Silver Book'

These Conditions of Contract are intended for use where one entity (the Contractor) provides a fully equipped facility ready for operation at the 'turn of the key'. The Employer is required to provide a fully descriptive document specifying precisely what is to be built and to what standards. In defining the Employer's Requirements, he may provide preliminary drawings, site data and technical requirements including specifications. The Employer's Requirements may also contain requirements for specified outputs from the completed facility.

This form of Conditions of Contract has not found favour in the construction industry, as the risk, both for time and money, which is allocated to the Contractor by the Silver Book is far greater than that allocated by the Yellow Book. The cost of preparing a tender offer is significantly higher than is the case using either the Red Book or the Yellow Book. Generally, there is a lack of reporting on any contracts that might be using the Silver Book forms.

The increasing use of Design, Build and Operate (DBO) projects (refer to discussion in Appendix E following) and the issue by FIDIC in 2008 of the Conditions of Contract for Design, Build and Operate projects (the 'Gold Book') have effectively eliminated one key type of project where the Silver Book might have been considered for use as a source document.

Appendix C
Other FIDIC Publications

(1) Short Form of Contract ('The Green Book')

In addition to the Red Book (CONS), the Yellow Book (P & DB) and the Silver Book (EPCT) already discussed, the Green Book completes the original 'Rainbow' suite of contract forms published by FIDIC in 1999. The Green Book is intended for repetitive engineering and building work of low value.

(2) Conditions of Contract for Construction – MDB Harmonised Edition (The 'Pink Book')

Increasingly, Multilateral Development Banks (MDB), such as World Bank, the European Bank for Reconstruction and Development, African Development Bank and others became concerned at the high levels of corruption, misuse of funds and labour abuses existing within the construction industry. Originally MDB were of a mind to develop their own contract forms which would incorporate provisions for a tighter control of funding in order to stamp out corrupt and fraudulent practices and would also provide better protection of workers engaged on funded projects.

The MDB and FIDIC agreed to co-operate and provide a form of contract that would fulfil the needs of the MDB and yet retain the standard FIDIC features which were familiar to those engaged in the international construction industry.

One important feature of the Pink Book is that many items previously intended to be included in the Particular Conditions are now included in the General Conditions.

The Pink Book is essentially a variant of the Red Book (CONS) and those familiar with the use of the latter will find little difficulty in the use of the Pink Book.

The Pink Book was originally issued in May 2005, revised in March 2006 and further revised in June 2010.

An Employer's and Engineer's Guide to the FIDIC Conditions of Contract,
First Edition. Michael D. Robinson.
© 2013 John Wiley & Sons, Ltd. Published 2013 by John Wiley & Sons, Ltd.

(3) Conditions of Contract for Design, Build and Operate Projects (DBO) (The 'Gold Book')

For some years the international construction industry has struggled to cope with the administrative detail arising from the increase in the number of DBO projects.

Each project has required the preparation of bespoke contract documents to meet the varying needs of the Employers, the financing banks and the Contractor, and this has proven to be an arduous time-consuming and expensive process.

The Gold Book brings together the functions of design, construction, operation and maintenance of a facility into one form of contract conditions and is specifically intended for 'Design, Build and Operate' projects, usually abbreviated to DBO projects.

The commissioning of a project is followed by operation and maintenance periods of 20–25 years duration. In that period the Contractor must meet stated operational targets and then hand back the project to the Employer at the end of the period of the concession in a pre-agreed condition.

A regular user of other FIDIC forms should have little difficulty in using the Gold Book.

(4) Dredger's Contract (The 'Blue-Green Book')

This Blue-Green Book is intended for use on contracts for dredging and reclamation work that is designed by the Engineer.

(5) Subcontract Forms

The previous edition of the Red Book entitled 'Conditions of Contract for Works of Civil Engineering Construction', 4th Edition 1992, was accompanied by a separate but complementary set of forms, relating to subcontracts. Both were effectively superseded by the issue in 1999 of the new Red Book 'Conditions of Contract for Construction' (CONS), followed by the issue of revised subcontract forms in 2011.

(6) Client/Consultant Model Service Agreements (The 'White Book')

The 4th Edition of this document was issued in 2006.

Appendix D
Employer's Claims under a CONS Contract

Sub-Clause	Title
4.18	Electricity, Water, Gas if stated in the Contract
4.19	Employer's Equipment and Free-Issue Material
7.5	Rejection (Defective Plant and Material)
7.6	Remedial Work
8.6	Rate of Progress (Contractor adopts revised methods that cause Employer additional cost)
8.7	Delay Damages (Contractor fails to complete on time)
9.4	Failure to pass tests on completion (only if Employer incurs additional costs)
11.4	Failure to rectify defects (Contractor fails to rectify)
13.7	Adjustments for changes in Legislation (reductions in cost to be refunded by the Contractor to the Employer)
15.3	Valuation at Date of Termination (Contractor's property valued by Employer on Termination)
15.4	Payment after Termination (Employer may claim losses and damage after Termination)
17.1	Indemnities (Employer claims for the cost of events for which he is to be indemnified by the Contractor)
18.1	General Requirements for Insurances (Employer makes claim if Contractor fails to insure)
18.2	Insurance of Works and Contractor's Equipment (Employer can claim refund if Contractor is unable to insure in accordance with the Contract)

An Employer's and Engineer's Guide to the FIDIC Conditions of Contract, First Edition. Michael D. Robinson.
© 2013 John Wiley & Sons, Ltd. Published 2013 by John Wiley & Sons, Ltd.

Appendix E
Contractor's Claims under a CONS Contract

Sub-Clause	Title	Time	Money
1.9	Delayed Drawings or Instructions	x	x
2.1	Right of Access to the Site	x	x
4.7	Setting out (errors)	x	x
4.12	Unforeseen Physical Conditions	x(c)	x
4.24	Fossils	x(c)	x
7.4	Testing	x	x
8.4	Extension of Time for Completion	–	x
8.5	Delay Caused by Authorities	–	x
8.9	Consequences of Suspension	x(c)	x
10.2	Taking Over of Part of Works	x	–
10.3	Interference with Tests on Completion	x	x
11.8	Contractor to Search	x	x
12.4	Omissions (by Variation)	x(c)	–
13.2	Value Engineering	x	–
13.7	Changes in Legislation	x(c)	x
14.8	Delayed Payment	x(c)	–
16.1	Contractor's Entitlement to Suspend	x	x
16.4	Payment on Termination	x	–
17.1	Indemnities (by Employer)	x(c)	–
17.4	Consequences of Employer's Risks	x	x
18.1	General Requirement for Insurances (if supplied by Employer)	x(c)	–
19.4	Consequences of Force Majeure	x	x
19.6	Optional Payment Termination	x	–
20.1	Contractor's Claims (procedural)	x	x

(c) = Contractor claim limited to Cost only

An Employer's and Engineer's Guide to the FIDIC Conditions of Contract, First Edition. Michael D. Robinson.
© 2013 John Wiley & Sons, Ltd. Published 2013 by John Wiley & Sons, Ltd.

Note: When notifying a claim in accordance with Sub-Clause 20.1, the Contractor is required to identify under which clause (or clauses) of the Contract he is making the claim. In addition he should make reference to Sub-Clause 8.4 if he is making claim for an extension of time.

Appendix F
Preparation of Interim Payment Certificates

General

An internationally tendered contract can be expected to provide for payments both in foreign currency and local currency. The ratio between foreign and local currency payments will be fixed in the Contract for the measured works. However, there will inevitably be a number of additional items and adjustments, where the ratio between currencies will differ from that applicable to the bulk of the currency.

The final appearance of the 'top sheet' of the Interim Payment Certificate will depend on the preferences of the Employer and the Engineer. For example, it may be preferred that the 'top sheet' provides separate columns showing the amounts included in the Contract (previous amounts), totals this month and total amounts to date. A horizontally drawn A3-sized document would be appropriate.

Payments to Nominated Subcontractors (including Provisional Sums)

A separate calculation sheet will need to be prepared for the payments due to nominated Subcontractors. This calculation sheet includes the percentage on-cost due to the Contractor. It is possible that the ratio between foreign currency and local currency will differ from that fixed for the Works.

Payment of Varied Works

The Employer and the Engineer will need to decide if payment for varied works shall be included in the general evaluation of the Works or shown separately. It is likely that there will be a unique ratio between foreign currency and local currency. Further, if the Employer has a restricted budget, he may require that the amounts expended are highlighted under this separate heading.

Valuation of Materials on Site

Since this item refers to the valuation of Materials on Site, it will be necessary to measure the amounts of Materials actually on Site at the end of the measurement period. The Contractor has to demonstrate that the Materials comply with the requirements of the Contract. Values for site manufactured Materials have to be negotiated.

An Employer's and Engineer's Guide to the FIDIC Conditions of Contract, First Edition. Michael D. Robinson.
© 2013 John Wiley & Sons, Ltd. Published 2013 by John Wiley & Sons, Ltd.

Adjustment for Changes in Legislation (Sub-Clause 13.7)

Increases or decreases in Cost arising from Changes in Legislation are limited to those costs arising from a change in the Laws of the Country. Consequently the adjustment will be valued entirely in local currency.

Adjustment for Changes in Cost (Sub-Clause 13.8)

Increases or decreases in Cost may arise from increases/decreases in the value of both foreign and local indices. The adjustment will therefore be made in both foreign and local currencies. Standard practice is to apply the fixed currencies ratio given in the Contract. There are a number of possible variants. In many instances suitable local indices may not be available. Consequently changes in cost of local labour and local materials may be evaluated against actual payrolls and invoices, leaving only the foreign adjustment to be calculated by the use of a formula proposed by FIDIC.

Deductions for Retention Money

The amount of retention to be deducted is calculated by applying the percentage given in the Appendix to Tender until the limit of the Retention Money is reached.

Return of Retention for the Works or Sections or Parts

Once a Taking-Over Certificate is issued, a portion of the Retention is to be returned. The Engineer is entitled to withhold certification of the estimated cost of outstanding work until it has been completed. The calculation of the amount to be returned in respect of Sections or Parts is a little more complicated than for the whole of the Works as indicated in the following table.

	Whole of the Works	Section of the Works	Part of the Works
	(%)	(%)	(%)
Amount of Retention Money	100	100	100
Repayment due on Taking-Over	50	40*	40*
Balance	50	60	60
Repayment due on expiry of the Defects Notification Period for a Section	-	40*	Payable only when parts comprise a whole section
Repayment due on expiry of the Defects Notification Period for the whole of the Works	50		

*These portions are calculated by dividing the estimated contract value of the Section or part by the estimated final Contract Price.

Summary of release of retention money

1 **Parts**
1.1 An initial 40% is due on taking over.
1.2 A second 40% is due once the last of the Defects Notification Periods of the parts comprising a Section expires.
1.3 The remaining 20% is included in the provisions of 2.3 below.

2 **Sections**
2.1 An initial 40% is due on taking over.
2.2 A second 40% is due once the Defects Notification Period for the Section expires.
2.3 The remaining 20% for all Sections is due once the Defects Notification Period forthe last Section expires.

3 **Whole**
3.1 The first 50% is due on taking over.
3.2 The second 50% is due once the Defects Notification Period for the whole of the Works expires.

PROJECT TITLE   CONTRACT NO......................
INTERIM PAYMENT CERTIFICATE No..........   FOR MONTH/YEAR...................
CONTRACTOR (Name)

                                                  Foreign Currency   Local Currency

     Measured Works

Add   Payment to Nominated Subcontractors
Add   Payment of Varied Works
Add   Payment of Claims
Add   Valuation of Dayworks
Add   Valuation of Materials on Site
Add   Changes in Legislation Cl. 13.7
Add   Changes in Cost Cl. 13.8

     Subtotal (1)
Deduct Retention Money (Limit …%)

     Subtotal (2)
Add   Return of Retention Money

     Subtotal (3)
Add   Advance Payment

     Subtotal (4)
Deduct Repayment of Advance

     Subtotal (5)
Deduct Amounts Previously Certified

     Amounts now certified for payment

Certified ....   Submitted by ....

Title/Position ....   Title/Position ....

Date ....   Date ....

Appendix G
Model Form for Submissions to the Engineer for Approval and/or Consent

PROJECT	**Serial No.**

ENGINEER: (Name)

CONTRACTOR: (Name)

SUBMITTAL TO THE ENGINEER FOR APPROVAL/ CONSENT/ INFORMATION

SUBJECT: Drawings/Method Statement/ Material Samples/ Test Results/ Plant Acquisition/ Q.A. Report/ Programmes/ Health and Safety
(Identify One)

TITLE: (Specify Title)

DETAIL: Drawing No./ Document No./ Sample/ Other

CLAUSE(S): ....

REF No.: ....

ATTACHMENTS: ....
....

DISTRIBUTION:

Submitted by .... Contractor	Re-submittal required .... Engineer
Date:	Date: ....
Re-submittal by .... Contractor	Approval/consent subject to corrections as noted .... Engineer
OTHER:	Approval/Consent .... Engineer Date: ....

An Employer's and Engineer's Guide to the FIDIC Conditions of Contract,
First Edition. Michael D. Robinson.
© 2013 John Wiley & Sons, Ltd. Published 2013 by John Wiley & Sons, Ltd.

Appendix H
Model Form of Engineer's Order for Varied Works

                                                    ENGINEER
                                                    (Address)

To: **CONTRACTOR**
       (Address)

c.c.: **EMPLOYER**
       (Address)

Contract Title:
Section:
Engineer's Order No.:

In accordance with Sub-Clauses 13.1 and 13.5* of the Conditions of Contract you are hereby ordered to carry out the following works to be valued under Sub-Clauses 12.3/13.5/13.6* or valuation given in letter (date/reference)*:

* Delete as appropriate.

Resident Engineer ....   Contractor...................................

Engineer..   Date of Receipt ....

Date ....

An Employer's and Engineer's Guide to the FIDIC Conditions of Contract,
First Edition. Michael D. Robinson.
© 2013 John Wiley & Sons, Ltd. Published 2013 by John Wiley & Sons, Ltd.

Appendix I
Model Form of Daywork/Daily Record Sheets

Sub-Clause 13.6 'Daywork' requires the Contractor to submit each day to the Engineer details of resources utilised.

Additionally, there are many instances in the Contract where the keeping (and agreement) of daily records is crucial if the Contractor is to be properly reimbursed for his efforts. This applies particularly to those events where the Contractor is entitled to payment of Cost. Further, there will be other occasions, particularly relating to claims and their quantification, where accurate records of actual events would be beneficial.

Following is a proposed standard format which can be varied to suit the requirements of an individual site. These daywork/daily record sheets should be colour-printed in groups of five and bound in sets of 100 (20 × 5).

Each set of five would have a unique sequential number. This would help identify records that are not signed, not presented or simply 'lost' in the system.

The top copy and one other would be taken by the Engineer and the next two copies by the Contractor's site office. These four copies would be perforated for separation. A fifth copy, unperforated, would be kept in the Contractor's field office responsible for producing the record sheets.

It may happen that the Contractor's supervisory staff are not fluent in the language of the Contract. Provided that Badge No./Fleet No./Material Codes are correctly recorded, together with the relevant quantities, the form can be conveniently completed by a junior staff member with the correct language skills.

The valuation of the individual sheets takes place in the Contractor's site office. The quantum, whether for daywork or other purposes, can be sent to the Engineer as part of the monthly application for an Interim Payment Certificate or as part of a claim presentation, accompanied by a copy of the original, signed daywork/daily record sheet.

An Employer's and Engineer's Guide to the FIDIC Conditions of Contract, First Edition. Michael D. Robinson.
© 2013 John Wiley & Sons, Ltd. Published 2013 by John Wiley & Sons, Ltd.

Date..................... DAYWORK / DAILY RECORD SHEET   Sheet Reference.....................

PROJECT ....   **SECTION** ....

DESCRIPTION...

REFERENCE (if any)...

	LABOUR					**EQUIPMENT**				**MATERIALS**		
	Badge	Name	Trade	Hours		Fleet No.	Description	Hours		Code	Description	Quantity	Unit
1					1				1				
2					2				2				
3					3				3				
4					4				4				
5					5				5				
6					6				6				
7					7				7				
8					8				8				
9					9				9				
10					10				10				
11					11				11				

CONTRACTOR: ....   ENGINEER:.....................

Distribution: Engineer: white+yellow
                       Contractor Office: green+pink
                       Site: blue – fast copy

Appendix J
Model Letters for Use by the Employer

Letter to the Contractor   c.c.: Engineer   EMP. 1.8

Sub-Clause 1.8 – Care and Supply of Documents

(Although this sub-clause requires the Employer to supply the Contractor with documents including Specifications and Drawings, in practice the Employer may delegate this task to the Engineer.)

(Quote)

In accordance with the provisions of Sub-Clause 1.8, Care and Supply of Documents, we herewith provide you with two copies of the following documents:

(1)
(2) (Provide full listing)
(3)

(Unquote)

Letter to the Contractor   c.c.: Engineer   EMP. 1.13

Sub-Clause 1.13 – Compliance with Statutory Regulations and Laws

(Quote)

We advise you that we have obtained (typically) a construction permit enabling work to commence.

(Unquote)

An Employer's and Engineer's Guide to the FIDIC Conditions of Contract, First Edition. Michael D. Robinson.
© 2013 John Wiley & Sons, Ltd. Published 2013 by John Wiley & Sons, Ltd.

Appendix J

Letter to the Contractor　　　　c.c.: Engineer　　　　EMP. 2.1

Sub-Clause 2.1 – Right of Access to the Site

First Letter

(Quote)

On (Date), at … hours, we intend to give you access to the Site and to hand over to you the whole of the Site (or hand over the following parts of the Site):

- (Provide details of the parts)

(And, if not already provided) Please ensure that the Performance Security is provided and that all required Insurances are in force prior to the date of the hand-over.

(Unquote)

Second Letter (in follow up)

(Quote)

We confirm that following a site inspection, the Site (and access thereto) was provided to you for the execution of the Works at … hours, on … (date).

or

We confirm that the following parts of the Site (and access thereto) were provided to you for the execution of the Works at … hours, on … (date):

(1)
(2)

Options:

1. Consider if it would be useful to attach a drawing or sketch to define the physical limits of the hand-over.
2. Exceptions

    The following minor areas/buildings are presently excluded from the hand-over and will be handed over as follows:

    (1) (Description) – available by (date)
    (2) (Description) – available by (date)

(Unquote)

Counter-signature for acceptance

....

Contractor's Representative

| Letter to the Public Authorities and others | c.c.: Engineer and Contractor | EMP. 2.2 |

Sub-Clause 2.2 – Permits, Licences or Approvals

It is not possible here to define all the various types of letters which the Employer may need to provide under the provisions of this sub-clause.

A topic frequently encountered is a need for the Employer to provide letters to Government departments in support of the Contractor's actions. Typically this would include letters to the customs authorities enabling the Contractor efficiently to import his Goods and Materials into the country and letters of support or explanation to local authorities who may be affected by the Contractor's activities.

| Letter to the Contractor | c.c.: Engineer | EMP. 2.4 |

Sub-Clause 2.4 – Employer's Financial Arrangements

The tender documents will invariably provide basic information of the Employer's financial arrangements. Queries are most likely to arise when the Contractor is required to perform additional works at a stage of the Contract when the stated source of financing is already exhausted.

A simple response to a request from the Contractor for clarification could be:

(Quote)

In response to your letter reference/data, you are advised that funding for the remaining/additional works is to be provided by ....

(Unquote)

Letter to the Engineer	c.c.: Contractor	EMP. 2.5

Sub-Clause 2.5 – Employer's Claims

Note: A full listing of matters which entitle the Employer to claim payment from the Contractor is provided in Appendix D.

Sub-Clause 2.5 does not provide a specific period in which the Employer is obligated to give notice of his intention to make a claim against the Contractor and states only that '*The notice shall be given as soon as practicable after the Employer became aware of the event or circumstances giving rise to the claim*'.

A typical letter would be:

(Quote)

In compliance with the provisions given in Sub-Clause 2.5 of the General Conditions of Contract the Employer hereby gives notice that he considers himself entitled to payment from the Contractor in respect of … (provide claim heading) in accordance with Sub-Clause … (refer to Appendix D).

(Unquote)

The above letter records only the Employer's entitlement. A follow-up letter should follow detailing with precision the amount claimed by the Employer for evaluation by the Engineer in accordance with the provisions of Sub-Clause 3.5, Determinations.

Note: Because of its importance, a separate draft model letter (EMP. 8.7) on the topic of Delay Damages is included

Letter to the Contractor	c.c.: Contractor	EMP. 3.1

<u>Sub-Clause 3.1 – Engineer's Duties and Authority</u>

Whenever possible, the Employer will have named the Engineer in the tender documents. However, circumstances may arise which oblige the Employer to name the Engineer after the Base Date.
The following letter is appropriate:

(Quote)

In accordance with Sub-Clause 3.1, Engineer's Duties and Authority, (name of Engineer) has been appointed as Engineer.
Details of the Engineer are as follows:

Name:

Represented by:

Address:

Address for Correspondence (if different):

E-mail:

Telephone:

Facsimile:

(Unquote)

Note: It is the duty of the Engineer to advise the Contractor of any delegation of his authority in accordance with Sub-Clause 3.2.

Letter to the Contractor c.c.: Engineer **EMP. 3.4**

Sub-Clause 3.4 – Replacement of the Engineer

(Quote)

We advise you that the current Engineer (name) will be replaced with effect from (date) by (name).
   Details of the replacement Engineer are as follows:

Name:

Represented by:

Address:

Address for Correspondence (if different):

E-mail:

Telephone:

Facsimile:

(Unquote)

Letter to the Contractor   c.c.: Engineer   EMP. 4.2

Sub-Clause 4.2 – Performance Security

(Quote)

The Performance Security (number) provided by (Provider) and sent to us under cover of your letter (reference) has been evaluated and found to be in accordance with the requirements of the contract.

(Unquote)

Note: Should the submitted Performance Security not be acceptable, then a similar letter, but one of rejection, is to be sent, preferably identifying the reasons for the rejection.

Letter to the Contractor   c.c.: Engineer   EMP. 4.10

Sub-Clause 4.10 – Site Data

Note: The Employer is required to have made available to the Contractor, as part of the tender documents, all relevant data in his possession prior to the Base Data.

It is a further requirement that the Employer shall make available to the Contractor all other relevant data that may come into the Employer's possession after Base Date. A typical letter would be:

(Quote)

In accordance with Sub-Clause 4.10 we herewith provide you with the following additional data:

(1)
(2)
(3)

The Contractor is responsible for interpreting this data.

(Unquote)

| Letter to the Engineer | c.c.: Contractor | EMP. 8.7 |

Sub-Clause 8.7 – Delay Damages

(Quote)

The Contractor has failed to complete the Works (or part of the Works) by (date) (Time for Completion). In accordance with the provisions of Sub-Clause 8.7, Delay Damages, the Employer gives notice that he considers himself entitled to payment of delay damages by the Contractor in respect of his failure. This notice complies with the requirements of Sub-Clause 2.5.

(Unquote)

Note: Unless the final period is known with exactitude, it is suggested that quantum of the claim could be delayed until the period of delay is final.

| Letter to the Contractor | c.c.: Engineer | EMP. 14.2 |

Sub-Clause 14.2 – Advance Payment

(Quote)

The guarantee provided for the advance payment (number) provided by (Provider) and sent to us under cover of your letter (reference/date) has been evaluated and found to be in accordance with the requirements of the Contract.

(Unquote)

Notes: (1) The Employer is required to provide the Contractor with an advance payment for mobilisation with the proviso that the Contractor provides an acceptable guarantee.
(2) Should the submitted guarantee not be acceptable, then a similar letter, but one of rejection, is to be sent, preferably identifying the reasons for the rejection.

Letter to the Contractor   c.c.: Engineer   EMP. 15.2

Sub-Clause 15.2 – Termination by the Engineer

(Quote)

In accordance with the provisions of Sub-Clause 15.2, Termination by the Employer, you are given 14 days notice that your contract (title/number) is terminated.
  Your contract is terminated for the following reasons:

(Select from sub-items (a) – (f) given in Sub-Clause 15.2)

(Unquote)

Notes: (1) Termination of the Contract is a most serious matter and should be subject to legal review before any notice of termination is issued to the Contractor.
(2) For defaults falling under Sub-Clauses 15.2 (e), Bankruptcy, and Sub-Clause 15.2 (f), Corruption, the notice of termination can be immediate, but this has to be stated so in the letter of termination.

Letter to the Engineer   EMP. 15.2

Sub-Clause 15.2 – Termination by the Employer

(Quote)

You have been notified by separate correspondence that Contract (name/number) of Messrs (name of Contractor) has been terminated with effect from (date).
  You are instructed to make a valuation of the Works in accordance with the provisions of Sub-Clause 15.3, Valuation at Date of Termination, taking into account the further requirements of Sub-Clause 3.5, Determinations.
  In addition, you are required to take delivery of any Goods, all Contract Materials and other design documents made for or by the Contract, to categorise the same and arrange for them to be delivered to the Employer in a manner and timing to be discussed.

(Unquote)

Note: Other specific matters, such as the Engineer's accommodation, vehicles, ongoing site security could also be addressed in these instructions or addressed in a separate letter.

Letter to the Contractor (only if required)   c.c.: Engineer   **EMP. 18.0**

Clause 18.0 – Insurances

Within the Contract Documents the Employer will have defined whether he will himself provide the required Contract insurances or whether he required the Contractor to provide the same. In either case the services of insurance specialists will be required to ensure that the contractual obligations of the Parties are correctly addressed.

There is no requirement for the Employer to approve insurance documents provided by the Contractor's insurers, since there is a risk of inadvertently affecting the risk distribution between the Parties. It is appropriate that the Employer advises the Contractor of any inadequacies of the Contractor provided insurance policy and request that they be amended accordingly.

Letter to the Contractor   c.c.: Engineer   EMP. 20.2

Sub-Clause 20.2 – Appointment of the Dispute Adjudication Board

(Quote)

We propose to appoint (name) as a member of the Dispute Adjudication Board. A copy of the curriculum vitae of (name) is attached for your examination.
   Your consent is requested.

(Unquote)

and

(Quote)

We consent to the appointment of (name – Contractor's member) as a member of the Dispute Adjudication Board.

(Unquote)

Letter to the Contractor   c.c.: Engineer   EMP. 20.4

Sub-Clause 20.4 – Obtaining Dispute Adjudication Board's Decision

(Quote)

We have received the Dispute Adjudication Board's decision (number/title).
   We are dissatisfied with the decision of the Board and required that the dispute be referred to arbitration in accordance with the procedures stated in Sub-Clauses 20.5 and 20.6 of the Conditions of Contract.

(Unquote)

Note: This notice is to be given within 28 days of receipt of the DABs decision. It is not necessary to explain the reason for non-acceptance in this response. If the non-acceptance is limited to one part of the decision, then the response should clarify matters.

Appendix K
Model Letters for Use by the Engineer

Introduction

This Appendix provides model letters for use by the Engineer primarily for formal correspondence with the Contractor.

These model letters do not distinguish between the letters written by the Engineer and those written by the Resident Engineer – all are referred to as letters to be written by the Engineer. The nature and scope of letters which will be written by the Resident Engineer will reflect the authority and powers delegated to him by the Engineer. The extent of this delegation will vary from organisation to organisation and from project to project. On larger and more complex projects the Engineer may retain to himself a direct role in the supervision of a project, whilst for a small routine project the level of delegation to the Resident Engineer may be substantial.

Consequently these model letters are shown in this Appendix as written by the Engineer. The reader is required to determine for himself which letters can be written by the Resident Engineer acting within the authority and powers delegated to him.

A substantial portion of site generated correspondence relates to routine site activities. The nature of this correspondence is diverse and its content and structure cannot be predicted. These model letters are intended to provide guidance on key contractual issues which, if not administered correctly in accordance with the terms of the Contract, can often have unintended consequences.

Finally, it is assumed that all letters written by the Engineer will be copied to the Employer if he is not the recipient.

It is also recognised that the Engineer will have an important role in the preparation of letters which are to be sent by the Employer. The Engineer will also be deeply involved in correspondence, report preparation and other activities connected with the work of the DAB and any arbitral proceedings.

An Employer's and Engineer's Guide to the FIDIC Conditions of Contract, First Edition. Michael D. Robinson.
© 2013 John Wiley & Sons, Ltd. Published 2013 by John Wiley & Sons, Ltd.

Letter to the Contractor   c.c.: Employer   **ENG. 1.8**

Sub-Clause 1.8 – Care and Supply of Documents

(Quote)

With reference to Sub-Clause 1.8 of the Conditions of Contract, we herewith enclose two copies of the Contract Documents comprising:

(provide listing)

Or

With reference to Sub-Clause 1.8 of the Conditions of Contract, we confirm having supplied you with two copies of the Contract Documents comprising:

(provide listing)

(Unquote)

Note: This letter is required only if the Employer does not make the required distribution.

| Letter to the Contractor | c.c.: Employer | ENG. 3.2(a) |

Sub-Clause 3.2 – Delegation of Authority by the Engineer

Alternative A

(Quote)

In accordance with the provisions of Sub-Clause 3.2 of the Conditions of Contract, you are advised that (name and title) has been appointed as the Engineer's assistant with immediate effect (or specific date).

Mr (name) will be referred to as the Resident Engineer (or other title).

The following duties and authority of the Engineer are delegated to the Resident Engineer:

(A full listing of these duties and authority are attached to this model letter for consideration.)

(Unquote)

Alternative B

(Quote)

In accordance with the provisions of Sub-Clause 3.2 of the Conditions of Contract, you are advised that (name and title) has been appointed as the Engineer's assistant with immediate effect (or specific date).

Mr (name) will be referred to as the Resident Engineer (or other title).

All duties and authority of the Engineer given in the Conditions of Contract are delegated to Mr (name), excluding (identify the duties and authority NOT delegated by reference to the relevant Clauses of the Contract).

(Unquote)

Refer to Letter ENG. 3.2(a)
Listing of Duties and Authority of the Engineer

Sub-Clause No.	Sub-Clause Title
1.5	Priority of Documents
1.8 (first paragraph)	Care and Supply of Documents
2.5	Employer's Claims (Giving of Notice)
3.5	Determinations
4.1 (4th and 5th paragraph only)	Contractor's General Obligations
4.4	Subcontractors
4.5	Assignment of Benefit of Subcontract
4.6	Co-operation
4.7	Setting Out
4.8	Safety Procedures
4.9	Quality Assurance
4.12	Unforeseeable Physical Conditions (Receipt of Notices)
4.16	Transport of Goods
4.17	Contractor's Equipment
4.19	Electricity, Water and Gas
4.20	Employer's Equipment and Free-Issue Material
4.21	Progress Reports
4.22	Security of Site
4.23	Contractor's Operations on Site
4.24	Fossils
6.5	Working Hours
6.7	Health and Safety
6.9	Contractor's Personnel
6.10	Records of Contractor's Personnel and Equipment
7.2	Samples
7.3	Inspection
7.4	Testing

Sub-Clause No.	Sub-Clause Title
7.5	Rejection
7.6	Remedial Work
8.1	Commencement of Work
8.3	Programme
8.4	Extension of Time for Completion
8.6	Rate of Progress
8.8	Suspension of Work
8.9	Consequences of Suspension
8.11	Prolonged Suspension
9.1	Contractor's Obligations
9.2	Delayed Tests
9.3	Retesting
9.4	Failure to Pass Tests on Completion
10.1	Taking Over of the Works and Sections
10.2	Taking Over of Parts of the Works
10.3	Interference with Tests on Completion
11.1	Completion of Outstanding Work and Remedying Defects
11.6	Further Tests
11.8	Contractor to Search
11.9	Performance Certificate
12.1	Works to be Measured
12.3	Evaluation
12.4	Omissions
13.1	Right to Vary
13.2	Value Engineering
13.3	Variation Procedure
13.5	Provisional Sums
13.6	Dayworks
13.7	Adjustments for Changes in Legislation

Sub-Clause No.	Sub-Clause Title
13.8	Adjustments for Changes in Cost
14.1(d)	The Contract Price
14.3	Application for Interim Payment Certificates
14.5	Plant and Materials Intended for the Works
14.6	Issue of Interim Payment Certificates
14.9	Payment of Retention Money
14.10	Statement at Completion
14.11	Application for Final Payment Certificate
14.13	Issue of Final Payment Certificate
15.1	Notice to Correct
15.3	Valuation at Date of Termination
16.3	Cessation of Work and Removal of Contractor's Equipment
17.4	Consequences of Employer's Risks (Notices)
20.1 (paragraphs 1, 4, 5)	Contractor's Claims (notices, records, detailed claims, particulars)

Letter to the Contractor ENG. 3.2(b)

(Quote)

<u>Absence of the Engineer from Site</u>

Please be informed that the Resident Engineer, Mr 'A', will be absent from Site from (date) to (date). Mr 'C' (name) will substitute for Mr 'A' in this period.

The duties and authority delegated to Mr 'A' by letter reference/date are transferred to Mr 'C' for the full period of Mr 'A's absence from Site.

(Unquote)

Letter to the Contractor　　　　　　　　　　　　　　　　　　　　　　　　　**ENG. 4.3**

Sub-Clause 4.3 – Appointment of Contractor's Representative

(Quote)

We refer to Sub-Clause 4.3 of the Conditions of Contract and request that you provide us with the name of your proposed Contractor's Representative, together with details of his qualifications and relevant experience.

We also require that you provide a statement confirming that he has full authority to receive on your behalf all directions and instructions from the Engineer which may be required to perform the Contract.

(Unquote)

Note:　The Contractor may already have introduced his proposed representative to the Employer and the Engineer at an early stage.

Letter to the Contractor ENG. 4.4

Sub-Clause 4.4 – Subcontractors

(Quote)

You are permitted to use the services of subcontractors named in the Contract without further consent. We request you to identify which of these named subcontractors you do intend to employ and for which works they will be engaged and to provide this office with the key data of the sub-contractor.

Should you have an intention to engage other subcontractors not named in the Contract, you are required to obtain the prior consent of the Engineer.

Your application for consent should be submitted well in advance of the engagement of the subcontractor and should provide:

- full name and address of the subcontractor
- company information
- full information concerning the experience of the subcontractor
- the name of the resident manager representing the subcontractor
- the scope and approximate valuation of the subcontract works to be sublet.

(Unquote)

Letter to the Contractor ENG. 8.1

Sub-Clause 8.1 – Commencement of Work

(Quote)

You are notified that the Commencement Date referred to in Clause 8.1 of the Conditions of Contract shall be (date).

You are required to commence the execution of the Works as soon as possible after the Commencement Date.

(Unquote)

Sub-Clause 8.1 requires that this notice is given within 42 days after the Letter of Acceptance is provided to the Contractor by the Employer. Sub-Clause 1.1.1.3 states that if there is no Letter of Acceptance, the date of issuing the Letter of Acceptance means the date of signing the Contract Agreement.

Letter to the Contractor ENG. 8.3

Sub-Clause 8.3 – Submission of Programme

(Quote)

Alternative A

In accordance with Sub-Clause 8.3 of the Conditions of Contract, you are required to submit a detailed time programme within 28 days of your receipt of the notice of Commencement Date. Your submission shall comply with the requirements of this Sub-Clause and shall include all supporting documents.

Please submit the programme not later than (date).

(Unquote)

Note: On receiving the Contractor's submission, the Engineer shall respond within a further period of 21 days. The Engineer is not required to approve or consent to the programme, but can advise the Contractor if his submission does not comply with the requirements of the Contract.

(Quote)

Alternative B

Under cover of your letter reference/date you have provided us with your intended programme of work and explanatory documents.

We have reviewed your submission and have the following observations to make:

(Provide details of observations)

Please take these observations into account and adjust your programme accordingly (or supply additional information) and re-submit the same to us as soon as possible.

(Unquote)

Letter to the Contractor ENG. 8.3

Sub-Clause 8.3 – Revision of Programme

(Quote)

We are of the opinion that the actual progress of the Works does not conform to the accepted programme.

In accordance with the requirements of Sub-Clause 8.3 of the Conditions of the Contract, you are required to provide a revised programme showing how the programme shall be modified to ensure completion of the Works within the stated time for completion.

(Unquote)

Note: Note the relationship between the request and the similar request made under the provisions of Sub-Clause 8.6, Rate of Progress.

Letter to the Contractor ENG. 8.6

Sub-Clause 8.6 – Rate of Progress

(Quote)

We are of the opinion that your rate of progress is too slow to enable you to complete the Works by the due date.

In accordance with the requirements of Sub-Clause 8.6, please provide details of your intended course of action to speed up the progress of the Works.

(Unquote)

Notes: (1) Note the relationship between this letter and a similar request made under the provisions of Sub-Clause 8.3.
(2) The impact of this letter would be significantly improved if it also makes reference to earlier letters on this topic, minutes of meetings and similar.
(3) Note that the FIDIC Guide states that this letter is not appropriate if the Contractor has an entitlement to an extension of time under the provisions of Sub-Clause 8.4.

Letter to the Contractor ENG. 8.8

Sub-Clause 8.8 – Suspension of Work

(Quote)

In accordance with Sub-Clause 8.8 of the Conditions of Contract, you are hereby instructed to suspend the Works (or Part of the Works consisting of ....) until further notice (or for a period of ...).

Throughout the period of suspension you shall continue with your contractual obligations to protect and secure the Works (or part thereof).

(Unquote)

Note: If the suspension arises as a consequence of an event for which the Contractor is responsible under the terms of the Contract, then he has no entitlement to additional payment and an extension of time. Conversely, if the suspension arises as a consequence of an event for which the Contractor is not responsible, then he may have a valid claim for additional payment and an extension of time for completion.

In his letter, the Engineer may choose to record the cause of the suspension or leave it to the Contractor to make a claim.

Letter to the Employer　　　　c.c.: Contractor　　　　ENG. 10.1(a)

Taking-Over Certificate for the Whole of the Works

(Quote)

In accordance with the provisions of Sub-Clause 10.1, the Contractor has provided a notice dated …, stating that in his opinion the whole of the Works will be complete and ready for taking over on (date).

The Engineer has reviewed the Contractor's notice and, in accordance with Sub-Clause 10.1, certifies that the whole of the Works was completed on (date) in accordance with the Contract, excepting for minor outstanding works and defects, which are listed in an annex to this letter, which will not affect the use of the Works for their intended purpose.

We shall now proceed to issue the Taking-Over Certificate to the Contractor with an effective date of (date as above).

(Unquote)

Notes:　(1)　It is assumed that this certificate will not be issued without the prior knowledge and agreement of the Employer, not least because he may have to make prior arrangements for security, staffing and other activities following the taking over.
　　　　(2)　The notification of the issue of the Taking-Over Certificate is provided in letter 10.1(c) following.

Letter to the Employer   c.c.: Contractor   ENG. 10.1(b)

Taking-Over Certificate for Section .... of the Works

(Quote)

In accordance with the provisions of Sub-Clause 10.1 of the Contract, the Contractor has provided a notice dated ......, stating that in his opinion the Section of the Works (describe) will be complete and ready for taking over on (date).

We confirm that the Section under reference corresponds to a Section described in the Conditions of Contract.

The Engineer has reviewed the Contractor's notice and, in accordance with Sub-Clause 10.1, certifies that the Section of the Works was completed on (date) in accordance with the Contract, excepting for minor outstanding works and defects which are listed in an annex to this letter, which will not affect the use of the Section for its intended purpose.

We shall now proceed to issue the Taking-Over Certificate to the Contractor with an effective date of (date as above).

(Unquote)

Notes: (1) If required, the precise description of the Section is to be provided in a separate annex.
         (2) See notes for Letter 10.1(a).

Letter to the Contractor   c.c.: Employer   ENG. 10.1(c)

Taking-Over Certificate for the Whole of the Works

(Quote)

Having received your notice under Sub-Clause 10.1 of the Conditions of Contract, we hereby certify that the Works were completed in accordance with the Contract on (date), except for minor snagging work and defects (which include those listed in the attached snagging list) and which should not substantially affect the use of the Works for their intended purpose.

(Unquote)

Note: The above text is taken directly from the FIDIC Contracts Guide.

Letter to the Contractor   c.c.: Employer   ENG. 10.1(d)

Taking-Over Certificate for a Section of the Works

(Quote)

Having received your notice under Sub-Clause 10.1 of the Conditions of Contract, we hereby certify that the following Section of the Works was completed in accordance with the Contract on the date stated below, except for minor outstanding work and defects (which include those listed in the attached snagging list) and which should not substantially affect the use of such Section for its intended purpose.

(Unquote)

Notes: (1) The above text is taken directly from the FIDIC Contracts Guide.
        (2) If required, the precise description of the Section is to be provided in a separate annex.

Letter to the Contractor ENG. 10.1(e)

<u>Rejection of Application for a Taking-Over Certificate for the Whole
(or a Section) of the Works</u>

(Quote)

Reference is made to your notice (reference/date) requesting that a Taking-Over certificate be issued for the whole of the Works (or Section ....) of the Works in accordance with the provisions of Sub-Clause 10.1.

It is the Engineer's opinion that further work has to be completed before the requested certificate can be issued. The outstanding work is detailed in an annex to this letter. Please advise us when this outstanding work is complete and ready for our inspection prior to your making a further application for a Taking-Over Certificate.

(Unquote)

Note: Sub-Clause 10.1 requires that the Contractor's application is responded to within a period of 28 days of receipt of the application by the Engineer.

Letter to the Employer   c.c.: Contractor   ENG. 10.2(a)

<u>Taking-Over Certificate for a part of the Works</u>

(Quote)

In accordance with the provisions of Sub-Clause 10.2 of the Contract, the Employer has requested that a part of the Works, namely (description) be taken over.

Whereas the Contractor has provided a notice dated (date) stating that a part will be complete and ready for taking-over on (date).

The Engineer has reviewed the Contractor's notice and in accordance with Sub-Clause 10.2 certifies that the part of the Works was completed on (date) in accordance with the Contract, excepting for minor outstanding works and defects which are listed in an annex to this letter, which will not affect the use of the part for its intended purpose.

We shall now proceed to issue the Taking-Over Certificate to the Contractor with an effective date of (date as above).

(Unquote)

Letter to the Contractor   c.c.: Employer   ENG. 10.2(b)

<u>Taking-Over Certificate for a Part of the Works</u>

(Quote)

We hereby certify, in the terms of Sub-Clause 10.2 of the Conditions of Contract, that the following parts of the Works were completed in accordance with the Contract on the dates stated below, except for minor outstanding work and defects, which include those listed in the attached snagging list:

    Description of Part   Date of taking over

(Unquote)

Notes: (1) If the description of the Part is complex, it is important that it is described with some precision in an annex to this letter.
           (2) The taking over is at the Employer's request. Consequently the Contractor has no right to make a formal application for a taking over.

Letter to the Employer   c.c.: Contractor   ENG. 11.9

Performance Certificate

(Quote)

The Defects Notification Period (or the latest Defects Notification Period) in respect of the Works expired on (date).
   The Contractor has

- completed and tested all Works including all work identified as outstanding at the date of issue of the Taking-Over Certificate
- remedied all defects
- supplied all Contractor's Documents.

The Engineer hereby certifies that on (date) the Contractor completed his obligations under the Contract.

(Unquote)

Letter to the Contractor ENG. 12.1

Sub-Clause 12.1 – Works to be Measured

(Quote)

The Engineer intends to measure (describe the item to be measured) on (date) at (time) hours.
   Please send a representative to assist the Engineer to make this measurement.

(Unquote)

Note: In most situations it would be expected that arrangements as noted above would be arranged verbally. However, there may be contractual reasons in some instances why a degree of formality is appropriate.

Letter to the Contractor　　　　c.c.: Employer　　　　ENG. 13.5(b)

Sub-Clause 13.5(b) – Nominated Subcontract for … (brief description)

(Quote)

In accordance with Sub-Clause 13.5(b) of the Conditions of Contract, you are instructed to enter into a Contract with (name/address of Subcontractor) for the execution of (brief description as above) or (supply of plant or materials or services) in accordance with their letter of offer dated (date), a copy of which is attached to this instruction.

This work will be carried out in accordance with the terms and conditions of the Contract between yourselves and the Subcontractor and will be measured and paid for in accordance with the Subcontractor's offer.

We remind you that in accordance with Sub-Clause 4.4, Subcontractors, you are responsible for the actions and performance of the Subcontractor.

Payment will be made to you in accordance with the provisions of Sub-Clause 13.5(b).

As discussed with you, the delivery dates and programme of execution of the subcontract conforms to your own programme of works and that you will comply with all your obligations under the Contract.

OR

Your placement of this subcontract order is deemed to represent your acceptance that the programme for the subcontract conforms to your programme of work.

Please provide us with a copy of your order and subcontract agreement as soon as it is concluded.

(Unquote)

Note:　There is general assumption that the subcontract would have been discussed by the Employer, the Engineer, the Contractor and the Subcontractor, particularly if there are clauses in the subcontract at variance to the clauses of the Contract. The Engineer's instruction to the Contractor should represent a confirmation of agreement between all parties.

Letter to the Employer ENG. 14.9(a)

Taking-Over Certificate for the Works

Release of Retention Money

(Quote)

In accordance with the provisions of Sub-Clause 10.1 of the Conditions of Contract, the Engineer has issued a Taking-Over Certificate for the whole of the Works dated (date).

In accordance with the provisions of Sub-Clause 14.9 of the Conditions of Contract, one half of the retention money amounting to (amount) becomes due for payment to the Contractor. This amount due is shown in an annex to this letter and will be included in the next Interim Payment Certificate.

(Unquote)

Letter to the Employer ENG. 14.9(b)

Taking-Over Certificate for Section (....) of the Works

Release of Retention Money

(Quote)

In accordance with the provisions of Sub-Clause 10.1 of the Conditions of Contract, the Engineer has issued a Taking-Over Certificate for the Section (description) of the Works dated (date).

In accordance with the provisions of Sub-Clause 14.9 of the Conditions of Contract, a pro rata release of retention (40%) is due. The amount due is shown in an annexure to this letter and will be included in the next Interim Payment Certificate.

(Unquote)

Note: If a Taking-Over Certificate has been issued for a part of the Works, the above model letter requires modification. Sub-Clause 10.1 is replaced by Sub-Clause 10.2 and references to 'Section' shall be amended to read 'part'.

Letter to the Employer ENG. 14.9(c)

Release of (Balance of) Second Half of Retention Money for the Whole of the Works

(Quote)

The Defects Notification Period in respect of the whole of the Works expired on (date).
   (Optional: The value of work outstanding at that date was [amount].)
   The (balance of the) second half of the retention money amounting to (amount) is now to be paid promptly to the Contractor.

(Unquote)

Notes: (1) The FIDIC Contracts Guide states that payment is due 'promptly', i.e. without reference to an Interim Payment Certificate. However, the Employer may require the Engineer to provide this document.
   (2) For clarity a calculation sheet could be provided as an attachment (refer to table included in Appendix F).

Letter to the Employer　　　　　　　　　　　　　　　　　　　　　ENG. 14.9(d)

Release of part of the second half of Retention Money
for Sections of the Works

(Quote)

The Defects Notification Period in respect of the following Section(s) of the Works expired on (date[s]).

(Description)

Forty per cent of the second half of the retention money amounting to (amount) should now be paid promptly to the Contractor.

(Unquote)

Notes:
(1) The FIDIC Contracts Guide states that payment is due 'promptly', i.e. without reference to an Interim Payment Certificate. However, the Employer may require the Engineer to provide this document.
(2) Sub-Clause 14.9 makes no reference to the return of the second half of retention money in respect of parts of the Works which are the subject of a Taking-Over Certificate.
(3) A summary of the provisions for the release of retention money is included in Appendix F.

Letter to the Employer   ENG. 14.9(e)

Release of remaining amounts (20%) of the Retention Money for Sections of the Works

(Quote)

The Defects Notification Period in respect of the last Section(s) of the Works (description if appropriate) expired on date(s).

The remaining amounts (20%) of the Retention Money for all Sections of the Works totalling to (amount) should now be paid promptly to the Contractor.

(Unquote)

Notes: (1) The FIDIC Contracts Guide states that payment is due 'promptly', i.e. without reference to an Interim Payment Certificate. However, the Employer may require the Engineer to provide this document.
(2) A summary of the provisions for the release of retention money is included in Appendix F.

Letter to the Contractor ENG. 15.1

Sub-Clause 15.1 – Notice to Correct

(Quote)

You have been instructed (describe how) to (describe the remedial work) and to date no action has been taken by you.

Consequently, in accordance with Sub-Clause 15.1 of the Conditions of Contract, you are hereby instructed to remedy the faulty work by no later than (date).

(Unquote)

Letter to the Contractor   ENG. 15.3

Sub-Clause 15.3 – Valuation at Date of Termination

(Quote)

Following termination of your Contract by the Employer on (date), the Engineer is required to proceed in accordance with Sub-Clause 3.5, Determinations, to agree or determine the value of the Works, Goods and Contractor's Documents and any other sums due to the Contractor for work executed in accordance with the Contract.

In order to commence the preparation of this valuation, you are required to send representatives to attend a preliminary meeting to be held in the Engineer's offices at (…) hours on (date).

Please ensure that your representatives are fully prepared for the meeting and bring with them appropriate documentation.

(Unquote)

Note: The Engineer should proceed expeditiously to prepare the valuation at Date of Termination and the meeting proposed above would provide the possibility that the Engineer could agree the valuation with the Contractor in an amicable manner.

Difficulties may arise particularly if the Contractor is insolvent. His key staff may quickly disperse, with the outcome that it will be difficult to obtain adequate representation from the Contractor.

Letter to the Contractor　　　　　　　　　　　　　　　　　　　　　　　　**ENG. 20.1**

Sub-Clause 20.1 – Receipt of Notice of Claim

Title: (see below)

(Quote)

We acknowledge receipt on (date) of your letter (reference/date), in which you give Notice of Claim in respect of...... (brief description).
   In accordance with the provisions of Sub-Clause 20.1, you are required to submit full and detailed particulars of the amount claimed and the extension of time due. These particulars shall identify the clauses of the Contract on which you rely on to substantiate your right to claim.
   We have titled this claim .... and given it a unique number .... which we request you to use in all correspondence.

(Optional:

Sub-Clause 20.1 requires that you maintain contemporary records in support of your claim. These records are to include:

[Example: details of manpower standing])

(Unquote)

Introduction to Indexes

In the preparation of the 'Rainbow' series of Conditions of Contract and the FIDIC Contracts Guide FIDIC provides an Index which sorts the contents of the various Clauses and Sub-Clauses according to topics and not necessarily in conformity with the printed formal titles of the Clauses and Sub-Clauses.

For example Sub-Clause 1.3 is titled 'Communications' and yet in the index the following references can be located (each with a reference to this Sub-Clause):

Addresses for Communications
Certificates, copies to be sent
Communications
Electronic Transmission of Communications
Notices, Addresses for Communications

There are a significant number of similar multiple references for other Clauses and Sub-Clauses.

The FIDIC Index system is undoubtedly very comprehensive and of considerable benefit to those who are not familiar with the contents of the FIDIC Conditions of Contract and have only key topic references with which to work.

In this book the original FIDIC index system has been expanded to provide appropriate reference to the full text of this book and yet retains the possibility of referencing the text of other related FIDIC documents, notably the FIDIC Contracts Guide, which use the same index system.

However, there are occasions when it would be convenient to have available an alternative index which would sort topics according to the clause numbering and descriptions used by FIDIC. An alternative form of index is provided for this purpose.

An Employer's and Engineer's Guide to the FIDIC Conditions of Contract, First Edition. Michael D. Robinson.
© 2013 John Wiley & Sons, Ltd. Published 2013 by John Wiley & Sons, Ltd.

Index of Sub-Clauses (FIDIC System)

	Sub-Clause	Page
Accepted Contract Amount, Sufficiency of the	4.11	22, 85
Access for Inspection	7.3	32, 97
Access Route	4.15	23, 88
Access to the Site, Right of	2.1	10, 76, 165
Additional Facilities (Right of Way)	4.13	22, 87
Addresses for Communications	1.3	5, 74
Adjudication Board	20.2	67, 141, 174
Adjustments for Changes in Cost	13.8	47, 118
Adjustments for Changes in Legislation	13.7	47, 117
Advance Payment	14.2	49, 119, 171
Agreement, Contract	1.6	6
Amicable Settlement	20.5	69, 144
Approvals, Permits, Licences or	2.2	11, 76, 166
Arbitration	20.6	70, 144
Assignment	1.7	6
Assignment of Benefit of Subcontract	4.5	20, 82
Assistance by the Employer	2.2	11, 166
Assistants, Engineer's	3.2	77
Authorities, Delays Caused by	8.5	33, 101
Avoidance of Interference	4.14	22, 88
Care of the Works	17.2	59, 131
Certificate, Application for Final Payment	14.11	52, 123
Certificate, Final Payment	14.13	53, 124
Certificate, Performance	11.9	41, 111, 194
Certificate, Taking-Over	10.1	38, 108, 189–193
Certificates, Applications for Interim Payment	14.3	50, 119
Certificates, copies to be sent	1.3	5, 74
Certificates, Interim Payment	14.6	50, 121
Claims, Employer's	2.5	14, 76, 167
Claims, General	20.0	140
Claims Procedure	20.1	67, 140, 203
Clearance of Site after Performance Certificate	11.11	41, 111
Clearance of Site after Taking-Over Certificate	4.23	25, 92
Commencement of Works	8.1	33, 100, 184
Communications	1.3	5, 74
Communications, Language for	1.4	5, 74

An Employer's and Engineer's Guide to the FIDIC Conditions of Contract, First Edition. Michael D. Robinson.
© 2013 John Wiley & Sons, Ltd. Published 2013 by John Wiley & Sons, Ltd.

Index of Sub-Clauses (FIDIC System)

Completion of Outstanding Work and Remedying Defects	11.1	40, 110
Completion, Statement at	14.10	52, 123
Completion, Time for	8.2	33, 100
Conditions, Unforeseeable Physical	4.12	22, 85
Confidential Details	1.12	8
Contract Price, The	14.1	49, 119
Contractor to Search	11.8	111
Contractor's Claims	20.1	67, 140, 203
Contractor's Design	4.1	18, 80
Contractor's Documents, Employer's Use of	1.10	7
Contractor's Entitlement to Suspend Work	16.1	57, 129
Contractor's Equipment	4.17	23, 89
Contractor's General Obligations	4.1	18, 80
Contractor's Liability, Cessation of	2.5	14, 76, 167
Contractor's Liability, Limitation of	17.6	61, 133
Contractor's Obligations: Tests on Completion	9.1	37, 106
Contractor's Operations on Site	4.23	25, 92
Contractor's Personnel	6.9	30, 95
Contractor's Personnel and Equipment, Records of	6.10	31, 96
Contractor's Representative	4.3	19, 80, 182
Contractor's Superintendence	6.8	30, 95
Co-operation	4.6	20, 82
Cost, Adjustment for Changes in	13.8	47, 118
Currencies for Payment of Variations	13.4	45, 115
Currencies of Payment	14.15	53, 124
DAB – see Dispute Adjudication Board		
Data on Conditions at the Site	4.10	21, 84, 170
Daywork	13.6	47, 117
Default of Contractor, Notice of	15.1	54, 125, 201
Default of Contractor: Termination	15.2	54, 125, 172
Default of Employer: Entitlement to Suspend Work	16.1	57, 129
Default of Employer: Termination	16.2	57, 129
Defective Work, Removal of	11.5	41, 110
Defects, Failure to Remedy	11.4	40, 110
Defects Notification Period, Extension of	11.3	40, 110
Defects, Remedying of	11.1	40, 110
Defects, Searching for Cause of	11.8	111
Definition of 'Nominated Subcontractor'	5.1	27, 93
Definitions	1.1	3, 74
Delay Damages	8.7	34, 102, 171
Delays Caused by Authorities	8.5	33, 101
Delegation by the Engineer	3.2	77, 177
Design by the Contractor	4.1	18, 80
Determinations by the Engineer	3.5	17, 78
Discharge	14.12	53, 124
Disorderly Conduct	6.11	31
Dispute Adjudication Board, Appointment of the	20.2	67, 141, 174
Dispute of the Adjudication Board, Failure to Agree	20.3	68, 142
Dispute Adjudication Board's Appointment, Expiry of	20.8	70, 144
Dispute Adjudication Board's Appointment, Failure to Comply with	20.7	70, 144
Dispute Adjudication Board's Decision, Obtaining	20.4	68, 142, 174
Disputes, Amicable Settlement of	20.5	69, 144
Disputes, Arbitration of	20.6	70, 144
Disputes, Failure to Comply with Dispute Adjudication Board's Decision on	20.7	70, 144
Disputes: Obtaining Dispute Adjudication Board's Decision	20.4	68, 142, 174
Documents, Care and Supply of	1.8	6, 74, 164, 176

Index of Sub-Clauses (FIDIC System)

Documents, Contractor's Use of Employer's	1.11	8
Documents, Employer's Use of Contractor's	1.10	7
Documents, Priority of	1.5	6
Drawing of Instructions, Delayed	1.9	7, 74
Electricity, Water and Gas	4.19	23, 89
Electronic Transmission of Communications	1.3	5, 74
Employer's Claims	2.5	14, 76, 167
Employer's Claims: Currencies of Payment	14.15	53, 124
Employer's Documents, Contractor's Use of	1.11	8
Employer's Entitlement to Termination	15.5	56, 127
Employer's Equipment and Free-Issue Material	4.20	24, 90
Employer's Financial Arrangements	2.4	13, 166
Employer's Liability, Cessation of	14.14	53, 124
Employer's Personnel	2.3	13
Employer's Risks	17.3	60, 132
Employer's Risks, Consequences of	17.4	60, 132
Employer's Taking Over, General	10.0	108
Engineer, Delegation by the	3.2	77, 177
Engineer, Instructions of the	3.3	78, 177
Engineer, Replacement of	3.4	16, 169
Engineer to act for the Employer	3.1	16, 77, 168
Engineer's Determinations	3.5	17, 78
Engineer's Duties and Authority	3.1	16, 77, 168
Environment, Protection of the	4.18	23, 89
Evaluation	12.3	43, 112
Evidence of Payments to Nominated Subcontractors	5.4	28, 94
Extension of Defects Notification Period	11.3	40, 109
Extension of Time for Completion	8.4	33, 101
Failure to Pass Tests on Completion	9.4	37
Final Payment Certificate, Application for	14.11	52, 123
Final Payment Certificate, Issue of	14.13	53, 124
Finances, Employer's	2.4	13, 166
Force Majeure Affecting Subcontractor	19.5	66, 139
Force Majeure, Consequences of	19.4	65, 139
Force Majeure, Definition of	19.1	65, 138
Force Majeure, Notice of	19.2	65, 138
Force Majeure: Optional Termination	19.6	66, 139
Fossils	4.24	25, 92
Frustration of the Contract	19.7	66, 139
Gas, Electricity, Water and	4.19	23, 89
General Provisions	1.0	3
Goods, Transport of	4.16	23, 88
Health and Safety	6.7	30, 95
Indemnities	17.1	59, 131
Inspection	7.3	32, 97
Instructions, Delayed Drawings or	1.9	7, 74
Instructions of the Engineer	3.3	78, 177
Insurance General	18.0	134, 173
Insurance Against Injury to Persons and Damage to Property	18.3	64, 136
Insurance for Contractor's Personnel	18.4	64, 136
Insurance for Works and Contractor's Equipment	18.2	62, 135
Insurances, General Requirements for	18.1	62, 134
Intellectual Property Rights, Claims for Infringement of	17.5	60, 133

… Index of Sub-Clauses (FIDIC System) … 209

Intellectual Property Rights in Contractor's Documents	1.10	7
Intellectual Property Rights in Employer's Documents	1.11	8
Interference, Avoidance of	4.14	22, 88
Interference with Tests on Completion	10.3	39, 109
Interim Payment Certificates, Application for	14.3	50, 119
Interim Payment Certificates, Issue of	14.6	50, 121
Interpretation	1.2	5
Joint and Several Liability	1.14	9
Labour, Engagement of Staff and	6.1	29
Labour, Facilities for Staff and	6.6	30
Language	1.4	5, 74
Law, Governing	1.4	5, 74
Laws, Compliance with	1.13	8, 75, 164
Laws, Labour	6.4	29
Legislation, Adjustments for Changes in	13.7	47, 117
Liability, Cessation of Contractor's	2.5	14, 76, 167
Liability, Cessation of Employer's	14.14	53, 124
Liability, Joint and Several	1.14	9
Liability, Limitation of	17.6	61, 133
Liability Unaffected by Insurances	18.1	62, 134
Licenses of Approvals, Permits	2.2	11, 166
Manner of Execution	7.1	97
Materials in Event of Suspension, Payment for	8.10	35, 104
Materials, Ownership of	7.7	32, 99
Materials, Payment for Unfixed	14.5	50, 120
Materials supplied by the Employer	4.20	24, 90
Measurement, Method of	12.2	43, 112
Measurement of the Works	12.1	43, 112, 195
Nominated Subcontractors General	5.0	26, 93
Nominated Subcontractors, Definition of	5.1	27, 93
Nominated Subcontractors, Evidence of Payments	5.4	28, 94
Nominated Subcontractors, Payments to	5.3	27, 94
Nomination, Objection to	5.2	27, 94
Notice of Intention to Deliver	4.16	23, 88
Notice to Correct	15.1	54, 125, 201
Notices, Addresses for	1.3	5, 74
Obligations, after Performance Certificate	11.10	41
Obligations, Contractor's General	4.1	18, 80
Omissions	12.4	43, 113
Other contractors	4.6	20, 82
Payment (by the Employer)	14.7	51, 121
Payment after Termination by the Contractor	16.4	58, 130
Payment after Termination by the Employer	15.4	56, 127
Payment, Currencies of	14.15	53, 124
Payment, Delayed	14.8	51, 122
Payment for Plant and Materials for the Works	14.5	50, 120
Payment in Applicable Currencies	13.4	45, 115
Payment to Contractor after Force Majeure	19.4	65, 139
Payment, Schedule of	14.4	50, 120
Payments to Nominated Subcontractors	5.3	27, 94
Performance Certificate	11.9	41, 111, 154
Performance Security	4.2	18, 80, 170
Permits, Licences or Approvals	2.2	11, 166

Index of Sub-Clauses (FIDIC System)

Personnel and Equipment, Records of Contractor's	6.10	31, 96
Personnel, Contractor's	6.9	30, 95
Personnel, Disorderly Conduct by	6.11	31
Personnel, Employer's	2.3	13
Personnel, Insurance for Contractor's	18.4	64, 136
Persons in the Service of Employer	6.3	29
Plant and Materials for the Works, Payment for	14.5	50, 120
Plant and Materials in Event of Suspension, Payment for	8.10	35, 104
Plant and Materials, Ownership of	7.7	32, 99
Programme	8.3	100, 185, 186
Progress, Rate of	8.6	34, 102, 187
Progress Reports	4.21	24, 90
Provisional Sums	13.5	46, 116, 196
Quality Assurance	4.9	21, 84
Records of Contractor's Personnel and Equipment	6.10	31, 96
Regulations and Laws, Compliance with	1.13	8, 75, 164
Rejection	7.5	98
Release from Performance under the Law	19.7	66, 139
Remedial Work	7.6	98
Remedy Defects, Failure to	11.4	40, 110
Remedying Defects	11.1	40, 110
Remedying Defects, Cost of	11.2	40, 110
Removal of Contractor's Equipment after Termination	16.3	58, 129
Replacement of the Engineer	3.4	16, 169
Reports on Progress	4.21	24, 90
Representative, Contractor's	4.3	19, 80, 182
Representative, Engineer's	3.2	77, 177
Responsibility for the Works	4.1	18, 80
Responsibility Unaffected by Engineer's Approval	3.1	16, 77, 168
Resumption of Work after Suspension	8.12	36, 104
Retention, Deduction of	14.3	50, 119
Retention Money, Payment of	14.9	50, 122, 197–200
Retesting after Failure of Tests on Completion	9.3	37, 107
Right to Vary	13.1	44, 114
Rights, Intellectual Property, in Contractor's Documents	1.10	7
Rights, Intellectual Property, in Employer's Documents	1.11	8
Rights of Way and Facilities	4.13	22, 87
Rights, Patent	17.5	60, 133
Risk and Responsibility	17.0	131
Risks, Employer's	17.3	60, 132
Royalties	7.8	99
Safety and Health	6.7	30, 95
Safety Procedures	4.8	20, 83
Samples	7.2	97
Schedule of Payments	14.4	50, 120
Search, Contractor to	11.8	111
Security, Performance	4.2	18, 80, 170
Setting Out	4.7	20, 83
Site, Clearance of	11.11	41, 111
Site, Contractor's Operations on	4.23	25, 92
Site Data	4.10	21, 84, 170
Site, Right of Access to the	2.1	10, 76, 165
Site, Security of the	4.22	24, 91
Staff and Labour, Engagement of	6.1	29
Staff and Labour, Facilities for	6.6	30

Index of Sub-Clauses (FIDIC System)

Statement at Completion	14.10	52, 123
Statement, Final	14.11	52, 123
Statement, Interim	14.3	50, 119
Statutes, Regulations and Laws, Compliance with	1.13	6, 75, 164
Subcontract, Assignment of Benefit of	4.5	20, 82
Subcontractor, Force Majeure Affecting	19.5	66, 139
Subcontractors	4.4	19, 81, 182
Subcontractors, nominated	5.1	27, 93
Superintendence, Contractor's	6.8	30, 95
Suspension, Consequences of	8.9	35, 103
Suspension due to Employer's Default	16.1	57, 129
Suspension of Work	8.8	35, 103, 188
Suspension, Payment for Plant and Materials in Event of	8.10	35, 104
Suspension, Prolonged	8.11	35, 104
Suspension, Resumption of Work after	8.12	35, 104
Taking Over of Parts of the Works	10.2	38, 109
Taking Over of the Works and Sections	10.1	38, 108, 189–193
Termination by the Contractor	16.2	57, 129
Termination by the Contractor, Payment after	16.4	58, 130
Termination by the Employer	15.2	54, 125, 172
Termination by the Employer, Optional	15.5	56, 127
Termination by the Employer, Payment after	15.4	56, 127
Termination, Optional: after Force Majeure	19.6	66, 139
Termination, Optional: at Employer's Convenience	15.5	56, 127
Termination, Valuation at Date of	15.3	55, 126, 262
Termination: Cessation of Work	16.3	58, 129
Testing	7.4	97
Test, Further	11.6	111
Tests on Completion – General	9.0	106
Tests on Completion	9.1	37, 106
Tests on Completion, Delayed	9.2	37, 106
Tests on Completion, Failure to Pass	9.4	37
Tests on Completion, Interference with	10.3	39, 109
Third Party Insurance	18.3	64, 136
Time for Completion	8.2	33, 100
Time for Completion, Extension of	8.4	33, 101
Time for Payment	14.7	51, 121
Transport of Goods	4.16	23, 88
Tribunal, Appointment of Dispute Adjudication Board	20.2	67, 141, 174
Unforeseeable Physical Conditions	4.12	22, 85
Unfulfilled Obligations	11.10	41
Valuation at Date of Termination	15.3	55, 126, 202
Value Engineering	13.2	115
Variation Procedure	13.3	115
Variations General	13.0	44, 114
Variations, Right to Vary	13.1	44, 114
Variations: Applicable Currencies	13.4	45, 115
Wages and Conditions of Labour	6.2	29
Water and Gas	4.19	23, 89
Working Hours	6.5	29, 95
Works and Contractor's Equipment, Insurance for	18.2	62, 135
Works, Contractor's Care of the	17.2	59, 131
Works, Measurement and Evaluation	12.3	43, 113
Works to be Measured	12.1	43, 112, 195

Index of Sub-Clauses (sorted according to FIDIC Clause numbering system)

Sub-Clause			Page
1	**General Provisions**		
	1.0	General	3
	1.1	Definitions	3, 74
	1.2	Interpretation	5
	1.3	Communications	5, 74
	1.4	Law and Language	5, 74
	1.5	Priority of Documents	6
	1.6	Contract Agreement	6
	1.7	Assignment	6
	1.8	Care and Supply of Documents	6, 74, 164, 176
	1.9	Delayed Drawings or Instruments	7, 74
	1.10	Employer's Use of Contractor's Documents	7
	1.11	Contractor's Use of Employer's Documents	8
	1.12	Confidential Details	8
	1.13	Compliance with Statutes, Regulations and Laws	8, 75, 164
	1.14	Joint and Several Liability	9
2	**The Employer**		
	2.1	Right of Access to the Site	10, 76, 165
	2.2	Permits, Licenses and Approvals	11, 166
	2.3	Employer's Personnel	13
	2.4	Employer's Financial Arrangements	13, 166
	2.5	Employer's Claims	14, 76, 167
3	**The Engineer**		
	3.1	Engineer's Duties and Authority	16, 77, 168
	3.2	Delegation by the Engineer	77, 177
	3.3	Instructions of the Engineer	78, 177
	3.4	Replacement of the Engineer	16, 169
	3.5	Determinations	17, 78
4	**The Contractor**		
	4.1	Contractor's General Obligations	18, 80
	4.2	Performance Security	18, 80, 170
	4.3	Contractor's Representative	19, 80, 182
	4.4	Subcontractors	19, 81, 182
	4.5	Assignment of Benefit of Subcontract	20, 82

An Employer's and Engineer's Guide to the FIDIC Conditions of Contract, First Edition. Michael D. Robinson.
© 2013 John Wiley & Sons, Ltd. Published 2013 by John Wiley & Sons, Ltd.

Index of Sub-Clauses (sorted according to FIDIC Clause numbering system)

4.6	Co-operation	20, 82
4.7	Setting Out	20, 83
4.8	Safety Procedures	20, 83
4.9	Quality Assurance	21, 84
4.10	Site Data	21, 84, 170
4.11	Sufficiency of the Accepted Contract Amount	22, 85
4.12	Unforeseeable Physical Conditions	22, 85
4.13	Rights of Way and Facilities	22, 87
4.14	Avoidance of Interference	22, 88
4.15	Access Route	23, 88
4.16	Transport of Goods	23, 88
4.17	Contractor's Equipment	23, 89
4.18	Protection of the Environment	23, 89
4.19	Electricity, Water and Gas	23, 89
4.20	Employer's Equipment and Free Issue Material	24, 90
4.21	Progress Reports	24, 90
4.22	Security of the Site	24, 91
4.23	Contractor's Operations on Site	25, 92
4.24	Fossils	25, 92

5 Nominated Subcontractors

5.0	General	26, 93
5.1	Definition of 'nominated Subcontractor'	27, 93
5.2	Objection to Nomination	27, 94
5.3	Payments to nominated Subcontractors	27, 94
5.4	Evidence of Payments	28, 94

6 Staff and Labour

6.1	Engagement of Staff and Labour	29
6.2	Rates of Wages and Conditions of Labour	29
6.3	Persons in Service of Employer	29
6.4	Labour Laws	29
6.5	Working Hours	29, 95
6.6	Facilities for Staff and Labour	-
6.7	Health and Safety	30, 95
6.8	Contractor's Superintendence	30, 95
6.9	Contractor's Personnel	30, 95
6.10	Records of Contractor's Personnel and Equipment	31, 96
6.11	Disorderly Conduct	31

7 Plant, Materials and Workmanship

7.1	Manner of Execution	97
7.2	Samples	97
7.3	Inspection	32, 97
7.4	Testing	97
7.5	Rejection	98
7.6	Remedial Work	98
7.7	Ownership Plant and Materials	32, 99

8 Commencement, Delays and Suspension

8.1	Commencement of Work	33, 100, 184
8.2	Time for Completion	33, 100
8.3	Programme	100, 185, 186
8.4	Extension of Time for Completion	33, 101
8.5	Delay Caused by Authorities	33, 101
8.6	Rate of Progress	34, 102, 187
8.7	Delay Damages	34, 102, 171
8.8	Suspension of Work	35, 103, 188

Index of Sub-Clauses (sorted according to FIDIC Clause numbering system)

	8.9	Consequences of Suspension	35, 103
	8.10	Payment for Plant and Materials in the Event of Suspension	35, 104
	8.11	Prolonged Suspension	35, 104
	8.12	Resumption of Work	36, 104
9	**Tests on Completion**		
	9.0	General	106
	9.1	Contractor's Obligations	37, 106
	9.2	Delayed Tests	37, 106
	9.3	Re-testing	37, 107
	9.4	Failure to Pass Tests on Completion	37
10	**Employer's Taking-Over**		
	10.0	General	108
	10.1	Taking-Over of the Works or Sections	38, 108, 189–192
	10.2	Taking-Over of Parts of the Works	38, 109
	10.3	Interference with Tests on Completion	39, 109
	10.4	Surfaces Requiring Reinstatement	-
11	**Defects Liability**		
	11.1	Completion of Outstanding Works and Remedying Defects	40, 110
	11.2	Cost of Remedying Defects	40, 110
	11.3	Extension of Defects Notification Period	40, 110
	11.4	Failure to Remedy Defects	40, 110
	11.5	Removal of Defective Work	41, 110
	11.6	Further Tests	111
	11.7	Right of Access	-
	11.8	Contractor to Search	111
	11.9	Performance Certificate	41, 111, 194
	11.10	Unfulfilled Obligations	41
	11.11	Clearance of Site	41, 111
12	**Measurement and Evaluation**		
	12.1	Works to be Measured	43, 112, 195
	12.2	Method of Measurement	43, 112
	12.3	Evaluation	43, 113
	12.4	Omissions	43, 113
13	**Variations and Adjustments**		
	13.0	General	44, 114
	13.1	Right to Vary	44, 114
	13.2	Value Engineering	115
	13.3	Variation Procedure	115
	13.4	Payment in Applicable Currencies	45, 115
	13.5	Provisional Sums	46, 116, 196
	13.6	Daywork	47, 117
	13.7	Adjustment for Changes in Legislation	47, 117
	13.8	Adjustment for Changes in Cost	47, 118
14	**Contract Price and Payment**		
	14.1	The Contract Price	49, 119
	14.2	Advance Payment	49, 119, 171
	14.3	Application for Interim Payment Certificates	50, 119
	14.4	Schedule of Payments	50, 120
	14.5	Plant and Materials Intended for the Works	50, 120
	14.6	Issue of Interim Payment Certificates	50, 121
	14.7	Payment	51, 121

Index of Sub-Clauses (sorted according to FIDIC Clause numbering system)

	14.8	Delayed Payment	51, 122
	14.9	Payment of Retention Money	52, 122, 197–200
	14.10	Statement at Completion	52, 123
	14.11	Application for Final Payment Certificate	52, 123
	14.12	Discharge	53, 124
	14.13	Issue of Final Payment Certificate	53, 124
	14.14	Cessation of Employer's Liability	53, 124
	14.15	Currencies of Payment	53, 124
15		**Termination by Employer**	
	15.1	Notice to Correct	54, 125, 201
	15.2	Termination by Employer	54, 125, 172
	15.3	Valuation at Date of Termination	55, 126, 202
	15.4	Payment after Termination	56, 127
	15.5	Employer's Entitlement to Termination	56, 127
16		**Suspension and Termination by Contractor**	
	16.1	Contractor's Entitlement to Suspend Work	57, 129
	16.2	Termination by the Contractor	57, 129
	16.3	Cessation of Work and Removal of Contractor's Equipment	58, 129
	16.4	Payment on Termination	58, 130
17		**Risk and Responsibility**	
	17.0	General	131
	17.1	Indemnities	59, 131
	17.2	Contractor's Care of the Works	59, 131
	17.3	Employer's Risks	60, 132
	17.4	Consequences of Employer's Risks	60, 132
	17.5	Intellectual and Industrial Property Rights	60, 133
	17.6	Limitation of Liability	61, 133
18		**Insurance**	
	18.0	General	134, 173
	18.1	General Requirements for Insurances	62, 134
	18.2	Insurance for Works and Contractor's Equipment	62, 135
	18.3	Insurance Against Injury to Persons and Damage to Property	64, 136
	18.4	Insurance for Contractor's Personnel	64, 136
19		**Force Majeure**	
	19.1	Definition of Force Majeure	65, 138
	19.2	Notice of Force Majeure	65, 138
	19.3	Duty to Minimise Delay	65, 138
	19.4	Consequences of Force Majeure	65, 139
	19.5	Force Majeure Affecting Subcontractor	66, 139
	19.6	Optional Termination, Payment and Release	66, 139
	19.7	Release from Performance under the Law	66, 139
20		**Claims, Disputes and Arbitration**	
	20.0	General	140
	20.1	Contractor's Claims	67, 140, 203
	20.2	Appointment of the Dispute Adjudication Board	67, 141, 174
	20.3	Failure to Agree Dispute Adjudication Board	68, 142
	20.4	Obtaining Dispute Adjudication Board's Decision	68, 142, 174
	20.5	Amicable Settlement	69, 144
	20.6	Arbitration	70, 144
	20.7	Failure to Comply with Dispute Adjudication Board's Decision	70, 144
	20.8	Expiry of Dispute Adjudication Board's Appointment	70, 144

WILEY-BLACKWELL

Other Books Available from Wiley-Blackwell

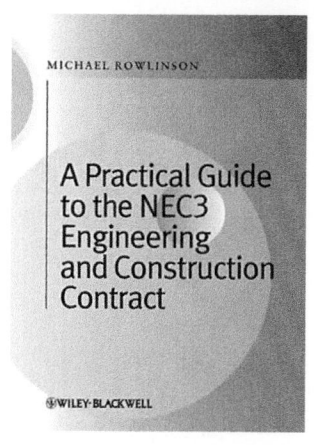

A Practical Guide to the
NEC3 Engineering and
Construction Contract
Rowlinson
978-1-444-33688-7

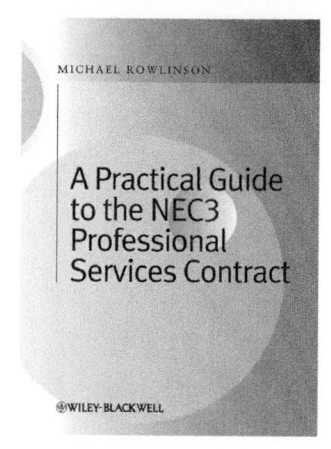

A Practical Guide to the
NEC3 Professional
Services Contract
Rowlinson
978-0-470-67234-1

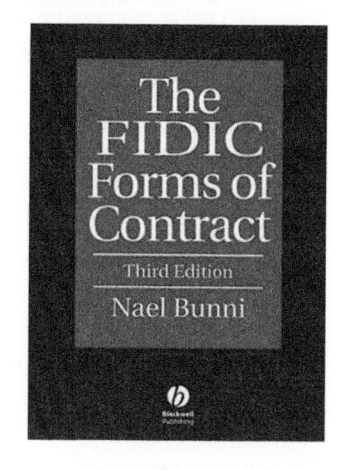

The FIDIC Forms of
Contract
Third edition
Bunni
978-1-405-12031-9

200 Contractual Problems
and their Solutions
Third edition
Knowles
978-0-470-65831-4

Construction Claims &
Responses:
effective writing and
presentation
Hewitt
978-0-470-65481-1

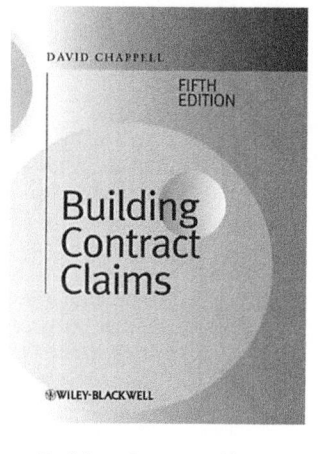

Building Contract Claims
Fifth edition
Chappell
978-0-470-65738-6

Forthcoming Books of Interest
The FIDIC Contracts: Obligations of the Parties
Hewitt
978-1-118-29180-1
Due to publish March 2014

www.wiley.com/go/construction

Printed and bound by CPI Group (UK) Ltd, Croydon, CR0 4YY